Vocabulary Energizers II:
Stories of Word Origins

by David Popkin, Ph. D.

DEDICATION

For Jonathan Sohn and Ian Romaine

ISBN 0-929166-02-7

Second printing: June 1991.
Third printing: November 1991.
Fourth printing: January 1995.
Fifth printing: January 1996.
Sixth printing: June 1997.
Seventh printing: June 1998.
Eighth printing: June 1999.
Ninth printing: June 2000.
Tenth printing: June 2001.
Eleventh printing: July 2002.
Twelfth printing: January 2003.

PRINTED IN THE UNITED STATES OF AMERICA

Hada Publications
2605 Belmont Boulevard
Nashville, Tennessee 37212

Contents

ACKNOWLEDGEMENTS

I would like to thank Ernest Heard, William Piersen, and Eric Youngquist for their careful critique of the manuscript. I would also like to thank Fisk University for a sabbatical that made the writing of this work possible.

D.P.

PREFACE

Vocabulary texts are too often dull compilations of words and their definitions. Students, initially interested in learning new words, come to associate vocabulary development with word lists, mechanical exercises, and rote memory. What a shame! Many words have fascinating origins and backgrounds. The history or etymology of a word provides a cultural context that helps imprint the word in our memories. Etymologies therefore serve as excellent mnemonic devices that deepen our understanding of a word's nuances and connotations.

For the past several years, I have emphasized narrative etymologies in a vocabulary development course that I introduced at Fisk University. Students learn that behind many vocabulary entries lurk enticing stories; rather than being numbed by word lists that ultimately destroy their incentive to continue vocabulary improvement beyond the confines of the classroom, they awake to the wonder of words. Their interest kindled, students become seekers rather than shunners of new words.

This book, like its predecessor *Vocabulary Energizers* (1988), is the offspring of my vocabulary course and has three aims: (1) to increase vocabulary, (2) to unveil the origins of words, and (3) to nurture an ongoing interest in words and their backgrounds. In order to help fulfill the third aim, I provide a bibliography of works that I have found especially rewarding and enjoyable in my search for the sources of words.

David Popkin

TO THE INSTRUCTOR

The format of *Vocabulary Energizers II* is ten uniform chapters. Each chapter contains ten core words with their etymological stories. After each story comes the category labelled "Synonyms." In this category I list several words. All but the last of these are easy synonyms for the core word. The last synonym is more difficult and is accompanied by its pronunciation. The first exercise at the end of each chapter is a passage in which the student fills in the blanks with core words. Next comes a matching exercise to reinforce both the core words and the difficult synonyms. I conclude each chapter with a word part from which five difficult but useful words are derived; students then must use these five words in the exercise sentences. Thus, each chapter contains twenty-five words (ten core words, ten difficult synonyms, and five words derived from a word part) for which exercises are provided. In addition, I often include the categories "Related Words" and "Contrasted Words" after "Synonyms." The related words are difficult synonyms or near synonyms for the core word; the contrasted words are difficult antonyms or near antonyms for the core word. Instructors can emphasize whichever of these words they wish. Since many words do not have exact synonyms or antonyms, the instructor can point out the nuances of meaning in the synonyms, related words, and contrasted words. Each chapter is independent from the other chapters so that the instructor is free to select the arrangement of chapters. Master exercises following the last chapter reinforce all of those words which previously were provided with exercises. These master exercises thus serve as a comprehensive review.

Chapter 1

1. Achilles' heel   6. desultory

2. stentorian   7. pariah

3. mnemonic   8. tawdry

4. fathom   9. pecuniary

5. serendipity   10. impecunious

1. *Achilles' heel* (uh KILL eez HEEL) *n.* weak point

The mightiest warrior in the *Iliad*, Homer's epic about the Trojan War—a war between the Ancient Greeks and Trojans—was Achilles. Strangely enough, the marriage ceremony of Achilles' parents caused the war. All of the important gods and goddesses were invited to the wedding with the exception of the goddess of discord, whose function was to cause trouble and conflict. She came anyway and threw a golden apple—with the inscription "for the fairest"—into the crowd. Hera (queen of the gods), Athena (goddess of wisdom and war), and Aphrodite (goddess of love) all claimed the apple. To settle the dispute, the three goddesses agreed to accept the judgment of Paris, a young Trojan prince. However, to make sure the verdict would be favorable, each of the goddesses bribed Paris. Hera offered to make him a world ruler, Athena promised to make him an unconquerable warrior, and Aphrodite offered him the most beautiful mortal woman in the world. A young, irresponsible playboy, Paris found Aphrodite's bribe irresistible and gave the golden apple to the love goddess.

Aphrodite then arranged for Paris to run away with the most beautiful woman in the world—Helen (who became known as the famous Helen of Troy). Unfortunately, Helen was married at the time to a Greek king. He summoned together other Greek kings and heroes to attack Troy in order to regain his wife. The resulting conflict of the Trojan War can thus be seen to have its origin in the marriage of Achilles' parents.

But why would a flaw or weak spot be named after Achilles, the most dreaded Greek warrior in this epic conflict? When Achilles was a boy, his mother dipped him in the River Styx so that his body would be made invulnerable by the sacred water. However, she failed to immerse the heel by which she held him. This heel was Achilles' one weak spot. In the tenth and final year of the Trojan War, Paris shot a fatal arrow into Achilles' heel. Thus, "Achilles' heel" has come to mean one's weakness, flaw, or vulnerable point.

I am an excellent student except for mathematics, my Achilles' heel. Occasionally an Achilles' heel may be located in another part of the anatomy, as in the fighter whose "glass jaw" is his Achilles' heel. The Achilles' heel of some loving parents is their inability to give stern punishment when needed.

Synonyms: weakness, flaw, defect, vulnerability (vul nuh ruh BIL uh tee)

Related words: infirmity, debility

Contrasted words: forte, mainstay

2. *stentorian* (sten TOR ee un) *adj.* very loud

Stentor, the Greek herald or official announcer of news in the Trojan War, would have no need of a megaphone, microphone, or amplifier. His voice was as loud as the combined shouts of fifty men. This voice ultimately proved his downfall because Stentor died from his effort to beat Hermes, the herald of the Greek gods, in a vocal contest. However, Stentor shouted loudly enough so that his name can still be heard in the English language. We refer to extremely loud-voiced individuals like some sergeants and football coaches as stentorian. A stentorian orator can make himself heard over the noise of a crowd. President Theodore

Roosevelt did not advocate using stentorian tones when he said, "Speak softly and carry a big stick."

Synonyms: booming, thunderous, thundering, resounding, roaring, sonorous (suh NOR us)

Related words: clarion

Contrasted words: inaudible, muted, subdued

3. **mnemonic** (nih MON ik) *adj.* assisting memory

Zeus, king of the Greek gods, lay nine nights with Mnemosyne, the goddess of memory. From this union came the nine Muses, the goddesses of the arts and sciences. Mnemosyne was the appropriate parent for the Muses because in the days before writing all knowledge depended upon memory. From Mnemosyne we get "mnemonics," the "art or technique of developing or improving the memory." A mnemonic device is a memory aid. For example, a mnemonic device or mnemonic ("mnemonic" can be either an adjective or a noun) that helps us remember the seven deadly sins is WASPLEG. Each of the letters of WASPLEG represents a sin: W = wrath (anger), A = avarice (greed), S = sloth (laziness), P = pride, L = lust, E = envy, G = gluttony (overeating). Each of the stories in this book serves as a mnemonic that aids you in remembering a word. Lest we forget, "amnesia" ("loss of memory") comes from Greek *a* ("not," "without") and *mnes* ("remember").

Synonyms: assisting remembrance, assisting recollection, assisting reminiscence (rem uh NIS uns)

Related words: assisting retention

Contrasted word: amnesiac

4. *fathom* (FATH um, the "TH" has the sound of "th" in "smooth") *v.*
    understand, figure out, penetrate the meaning of

Our word "fathom" derives form Old English *faethm*, a measure of the
length of outstretched arms. Our nautical term "fathom"—a measurement of six feet—thus comes from the Old English word for arm span.
By extension, this measurement of a water's depth came to mean "to
get to the bottom of" a situation or condition, thus to penetrate deeply
enough to understand and unravel a mystery or problem. Samuel
Clemens, the author of *Tom Sawyer* and *Huckleberry Finn*, chose as his
pseudonym or pen name "Mark Twain," a river term signifying that the
water is two fathoms or twelve feet deep.

   Few of us can fathom developments in modern physics; this field
is unfathomable or beyond the understanding of most people. No
matter how carefully I try to account for my expenses, I am unable to
fathom where all my money goes. The philosopher Friedrich Nietzche
(1844-1900) described his country with this sexist remark: "The Ger-
mans are like women, you can scarcely ever fathom their depths—they
haven't any."

Synonyms: know, grasp, comprehend (kom prih HEND)

Related words: apprehend, discern, divine

Contrasted words: misconstrue, misapprehend, misconceive

5. *serendipity* (ser un DIP uh tee) *n.* ability to make lucky discoveries
    by chance or accident.

The English politician and writer Horace Walpole (1717-1797) is best
known for his novel *The Castle of Otranto*. This work became the model
for future Gothic novels—tales suffused with mystery, dread, and the
supernatural, often set against an old, decaying, or medieval back-
ground—Mary Shelley's *Frankenstein* being perhaps the most famous.
In addition to originating the Gothic novel, Walpole coined the word
"serendipity" based upon a Persian fairy tale, "The Three Princes of
Serendip," whose three heroes Walpole described as "always making
discoveries . . . . of things they were not in quest of." Serendip was the

old Arabic name for Sri Lanka (formerly Ceylon). "Serendipity" has remained in our language as a wonderful word for a lucky accident. The British biologist Sir Alexander Fleming came upon penicillin by serendipity when he discovered in his laboratory that a bit of penicillin mold had accidentally fallen and destroyed the surrounding bacteria. We all know of Columbus' serendipitous discovery of the Americas while searching for a route to Asia.

Synonyms: chance, fortuity (for TOO uh tee)

Related words: happenstance, fortuitousness

6. *desultory* (DES ul tor ee) *adj.* random, unmethodical, aimless

Desultors—from Latin *de* ("from") and *salire* ("jump")—were ancient Roman acrobats who leaped from one galloping horse to another. Today, anyone who jumps from one thing to another without any design or purpose acts desultorily.

The efficient executive who plans every movement of his day is certainly no desultory worker; however, he fumes at the desultory habits of his disorganized son who cannot concentrate on any one task for long and never formulates any clear goals. Anthony Trollope, English novelist and contemporary of Charles Dickens, habitually rose at 5:30 a.m. and would proceed to write at the pace of 250 words every quarter of an hour for approximately three hours; Trollope's methodical, disciplined writing habits were the antithesis or opposite of desultoriness.

Synonyms: irregular, unsystematic, unplanned, rambling, haphazard (hap HAZ urd)

Related words: digressing, discursive, cursory, erratic, mercurial, capricious

Contrasted words: diligent, persevering, assiduous, sedulous

7. *pariah* (pur RYE uh) *n.* social outcast

About 3500 years ago Aryan invaders imposed a caste system on India dividing the population into permanent social groups, with the priests at the top and the common laborers at the bottom. Lowest of all were the outcasts or untouchables who did not belong to any caste. One remained for life in the caste of one's birth and could not marry someone from another caste. Within this rigid social stratification, the *Paraiyar*—who traditionally beat the drum (*parai* is "drum" in the Indian language of Tamil) at certain festivals—became a class of lowly field hands. When the British came to India, they took many of their household servants from the *Paraiyar* and began to pronounce the caste's name as "Pariah." Since they looked down on the Pariah, the British indiscriminately used "pariah" to describe the low castes, outcastes or untouchables, and eventually any lowlife that was despised or rejected by society. Interestingly, in medieval Europe lepers had to beat two sticks together to warn others to get away from them. Thus these European outcasts or pariahs were in a sense drummers as were the Indian *Paraiyar*.

The boy who informed the teacher about the bad behavior of the class in her absence became a pariah shunned by his classmates. Caught at cheating, the card player became a pariah among professional gamblers. Because of his many scandalous love affairs, including a relationship with his half sister, the English Romantic poet Lord Byron became a pariah who fled his homeland.

Synonyms: outcast, unacceptable person, persona non grata (pur SO nuh non GRAH tuh)

Related words: ostracized person, reprobate

Contrasted words: bigwig, luminary, cynosure

8. *tawdry* (TAW dree) *adj.* showy and cheap

In seventh- century England, a woman named Etheldreda fled from an undesirable marriage to become a nun. She enjoyed wearing ornamental chains and laces around her neck as a girl, and attributed a throat tumor in later life to this early fashionable practice. After Etheldreda died, her name eventually became shortened to Audry, and she attained sainthood. To honor her, an annual fair arose in the town of her monastery. Particularly marketable items at these fairs were scarves and necklaces known as "St. Audrey's laces" in recognition of the saint's youthful, fashionable behavior. Through the years these ornaments deteriorated in quality, and "Saint Audrey's lace" changed in pronunciation to "Sin t'Audrey lace" and eventually to "Tawdry lace." By its association with an inferior product, "tawdry" took on the general meaning of "flashily worthless" and "vulgar."

A tawdry dress would be inappropriate at an elegant, formal ball. Mary's conservatively correct parents stared with disgust at her friend's tawdry clothes. The candidate will never get elected if the press releases the sleazy, tawdry details of his personal life.

Synonyms: tasteless, vulgar, flashy, gaudy (GAW dee)

Related words: garish, meretricious

9. *pecuniary* (pih CUE nee er ee) *adj.* relating to money

10. *impecunious* (im pih CUE nee us) *adj.* having little or no money; poor

In many ancient barter or trade societies, before money became commonplace, one's livestock (cattle, sheep, goats) was a measure of one's wealth. *Pecu*, the Latin word for cattle or farm animals, therefore came to be associated with wealth, then money, and eventually entered English as "pecuniary," meaning "having to do with money." Of course, if a person was "without" (*im*) "cattle" (*pecu*), that person would be considered poor—hence our word "impecunious" for "poor" or "without money." Interestingly, the word "peculiar" also ultimately derives from *pecu* since Latin *peculiaris* meant the cattle or wealth that is particularly or peculiarly one's own. The smell of cattle can also be detected in our word "fee," derived from Old English *feoh* ("cattle," "property").

If you do not budget your money carefully, you will have pecuniary problems and find yourself impecunious. Many an impecunious loafer dreams of becoming a pecuniary marvel like Rockefeller or Donald Trump. Just as Charles Dickens in *A Christmas Carol* created the immortal characters of the pecuniarily successful Ebenezer Scrooge and his impecunious clerk Bob Cratchet, so did Walt Disney's cartoonist

Carl Barks delight us with encounters between the pecuniary wizard Uncle Scrooge and his impecunious nephew Donald Duck.

Synonyms for "pecuniary": financial, monetary (MON uh ter ee)

Related words for "pecuniary": fiscal, economic

Synonyms for "impecunious": penniless, indigent (IN dih junt)

Related words for "impecunious": destitute, insolvent, impoverished, penurious

Contrasted words for "impecunious": affluent, lucrative, opulent, solvent

Working With Words

Fill in each blank with the appropriate word from the following list:

impecunious	tawdry
desultory	pariah
stentorian	serendipity
pecuniary	Achilles' heel
fathom	mnemonic

Each word must be used only once.

Until her junior year at Academic High, Cindy Rella hated school. A (1)_____*desultory*_____ student, she would randomly jump from one subject to another without taking enough time or effort to (2) _____*fathom*_____ anything fully. To compensate for her poor academic performance, Cindy sought attention and approval by trying to dress fashionably. Unfortunately, her (3)_____*impecunious*_____ parents could not provide her with the latest designer fashions so that Cindy's attempts at style resulted in a cheap, (4)_____*tawdry*_____ appearance. Feeling the disapproval of her teachers and classmates, Cindy suffered loneliness and isolation as only a (5)_____*pariah*_____ could. When things looked their bleakest, suddenly a substitute teacher—Mrs. Farley-Gotmather—appeared in her history class. Even if Cindy had been a superior student in her other subjects, history would have remained her special weakness, her (6)_____*heel*_____, for she could never remember the required names and dates. At first, Cindy quivered as Mrs. Farley-Gotmather boomed in her (7)_____*stentorian*_____ voice the day's assignment. However, Mrs. Farley-Gotmather knew Cindy's deficiency and was determined to help the dejected girl. After class, Mrs. Farley-Gotmather tutored Cindy in (8)_____*mnemonic*_____ aids and systems to improve the memory. Inspired by the kindly help of Mrs. Farley- Gotmather, whom she had discovered by (9)_____*serendipity*_____ that lucky day when the regular history teacher failed to appear, Cindy Rella became an "A" student. She won a full scholarship to the college of her choice, thus removing the (10)_____*pecuniary*_____ barrier that could not be overcome by her family's finances. Today, Cindy Rella is the attractive, stylish president of one of the nation's most wealthy corporations—

the company noted for training the memories of business executives, Mnemonics, Inc.— whose motto states, "We won't let you forget to be a success."

II. Match the word on the left with its synonyms.

_____1. pariah   a. monetary, financial

_____2. impecunious   b. gaudy, vulgar

_____3. desultory   c. indigent, poor

_____4. Achilles' heel   d. fortuity, chance

_____5. pecuniary   e. comprehend, understand

_____6. tawdry   f. persona non grata, outcast

_____7. mnemonic   g. sonorous, loud

_____8. serendipity   h. vulnerability, weakness

_____9. fathom   i. haphazard, aimless

___10. stentorian   j. assisting reminiscence, assisting memory

III. Word Part: ARCH—ruler (architect)

monarch (MON urk) *n.* ruler or person who holds a dominant position, especially a hereditary ruler like a king, queen, emperor or sultan

anarchy (AN ur kee) *n.* absence of government or law; confusion, disorder

hierarchy (HY uh rar kee) *n.* person or things arranged in a graded series or rank

matriarch (MAY tree ark) *n.* woman who rules a family, clan, tribe or group

patriarch (PAY tree ark) *n.* father or leader of a family or group; dignified old man

Using each of the five ARCH words only once, complete the following sentences.

1. Lena Elder, the grandmother in Lorraine Hansberry's play *A Raisin in the Sun*, is the domineering, enduring, and loving __matriarch__ of her family.

2. Abraham is a __patriarch__ of the Hebrews in the Old Testament.

3. W. B. Yeats prophesies the breakdown of civilization in his poem "The Second Coming":

> Things fall apart; the center cannot hold;
> Mere __anarchy__ is loosed upon the world.

4. Babe Ruth, known as the "Sultan of Swat," could be described as a baseball __monarch__.

5. The Pope is the head of the Roman Catholic __hierarchy__.

Chapter 2

1. Spartan
2. gadfly
3. homage
4. spurn
5. pedigree

6. pittance
7. preposterous
8. macabre
9. farce
10. bombast

1. *Spartan* (SPAR tun) *adj.* severe, rigorous, disciplined

Life in Sparta, an ancient Greek city-state, was much like boot camp or basic training. Spartans survived on simple food and the barest minimum of clothing and shelter. Their daily routine included vigorous exercise and military training. To eliminate weaklings, Spartans even killed deformed or unhealthy infants.

An early Spartan king demonstrated his extreme self-discipline when he and his soldiers were about to die of thirst. The king promised to give over his entire treasure to the enemy's leader provided that the king and his men all receive water from a spring guarded by the enemy. Before allowing his men to quench their thirst, the king declared that anyone who refrained from drinking would be the new king. So parched were his men that none could resist gulping the water. However, the king himself passed the stream without tasting one drop of water. True to the narrowest interpretation of his agreement, the king—who had not drunk—therefore refused to yield his treasures to the enemy's leader after succeeding to refresh his warriors. This king's famous great-grandson Lycurgus, known as the creator of Sparta's laws, also revealed his capacity for self-control when he made the Spartan citizens promise that they would obey his laws until he returned from a visit to the oracle of Delphi, a place where the god Apollo presumably answered one's questions. After arriving at Delphi, King Lycurgus refused to eat, starving himself to death and thus insuring that his fellow citizens would perpetually observe his laws. Because of their reputation for discipline and enduring hardships, the Spartans lent their name to describe vigorous self-denial and a severely simple lifestyle.

By following a Spartan regimen of diet and exercise, I managed to lose thirty pounds in a month. Rocky Marciano, the only heavyweight boxing champion to retire with a perfect record (49-0, with 43 knockouts) would isolate himself weeks before fights so he could Spartanly train to reach his peak. "Spartan" can also be a noun as when we say a brave, uncomplaining person is a true Spartan.

Synonyms: self-denying, plain, spare, restrained, strict, stern, austere (aw STEER)

Related words: abstemious, abstinent, ascetic, stringent, frugal

Contrasted words: lavish, self-indulgent, hedonistic, sybaritic

2. *gadfly* (GAD fly)   *n.*   person who continually annoys others

Old Norse *gaddr* meant "spike." A gadfly, commonly known as a horsefly, is a large fly that spikes or stings cattle and horses. The meaning of "gadfly" has metaphorically evolved to refer to a persistently annoying person, especially one who tries to sting or arouse others to action. Perhaps the most famous of all gadflies was the ancient Greek philosopher Socrates. In his famous trial where he defended himself against the charge of corrupting the youth of Athens, Socrates referred to himself as a gadfly and to Athens as a great steed. The philosopher felt his purpose was to sting the conscience of the city and rouse his countrymen to moral action. Socrates began his career as a moral gadfly when told by a friend that the oracle of Delphi (voice of the god Apollo) had declared Socrates the wisest of men. Socrates did not feel particularly wise, so he went around cross-examining craftsmen, poets, and politicians to see if the oracle erred and perhaps someone else was wiser. Employing his scalpel-like intellect to dissect the opinion of others, Socrates discovered that no one indeed knew more. The only difference was that others were not aware of their ignorance and thought they knew something whereas Socrates himself knew that he knew nothing. He therefore concluded that the oracle must have meant that Socrates was the wisest of men because he alone knew the limits of his knowledge. Martin Luther King, Jr., holder of a Ph.D. in philosophy from Boston University and a great admirer of Socrates, roused the conscience of our nation in his role as gadfly for civil rights. While some gadflies may be restless, critical, and annoying to no meaningful end, humanity sorely needs more gadflies like Socrates and King.

Synonyms: critic, pest, faultfinder, goad (rhymes with "toad" and can be a noun or verb)

3. *homage* (HOM ij) *n.* action showing respect and honor

Feudalism was a military and political system in medieval Europe in which a warrior swore loyalty to his lord and in turn would be protected by the lord. In a formal ceremony, the warrior knelt unarmed and bareheaded while placing his hands between those of the lord. The warrior swore to use his hands and his weapons only for the ruler. This warrior would then become a "vassal" of the lord and receive a gift of land in return for military support. Since the vassal or warrior thus became the "man" (from French *homme*, ultimately from Latin *homo*) of the lord, this ceremony was called *homage*. Although we are no longer in the Middle Ages, we still pay homage to anyone we greatly respect or admire. Since "imitation is the sincerest form of flattery," we show homage when we model ourselves after our heroes. Baseball pays homage to great ballplayers with the Hall of Fame, Hollywood pays homage to its performers with the Academy Award, and the world pays homage to humanity's outstanding contributors with the Nobel prize.

Synonyms: honor, admiration, esteem, reverence, tribute (TRIB yoot)

Related words: deference, obeisance, veneration

Contrasted words: irreverence, contempt, disdain, scorn

4. *spurn* (SPURN) *v.* scornfully refuse or reject

Old English *spurnan* meant "kick." Shakespeare uses this meaning of "spurn" when he has Shylock, the Jewish moneylender in *The Merchant of Venice*, express his rage and resentment at being rudely handled by the merchant Antionio who has asked him for a loan:

> Fair sir, you [Antonio] spit on me on Wednesday last,
> You spurned me such a day, another time
> You called me dog; and for these courtesies
> I'll lend you thus much moneys?...
> You that did void your rheum [spit] upon my beard
> And foot me as you spurn a stranger cur [dog]
> Over your threshold!

"Spurn" still kicks where it hurts when the boy or girl of our dreams spurns us. The innovative filmmaker Spike Lee contemptuously rejects and spurns the shallow Hollywood stereotypes of Blacks.

Synonyms: scorn, repel, despise, decline, dismiss, repudiate (rih PYOO dee ate, PYOO rhymes with "few" and "blue")

Related words: disdain, rebuff, contemn, repulse

Contrasted words: crave

5. *pedigree* (PED uh gree) *n.* ancestry or record of ancestry, line of descent

During the Middle Ages noblemen had to substantiate their claims to an inheritance or title by proving their ancestry. The scholars they employed to trace their ancestry compiled genealogical charts or family trees that used a wavering three-line symbol to show descent. Since this symbol resembled the imprint of the foot of a crane (a long-legged and long-necked bird resembling a stork), the symbol was called *pied de grue* (*pied* = "foot," *de* = "of," *grue* = "crane") in French, the court language of many kingdoms at the time. *Pied de grue* also became the name for the historical family chart, and the word entered our English language in the fifteenth century. Through a series of spelling transformations, *pied de grue* became "pedigree," meaning "ancestry" or a "genealogical table showing one's descent." The Daughters of the American Revolution is a society of women who trace their pedigree back to persons who helped establish American independence. A pedigreed dog is a purebred whose papers show its line of descent. Heathcliff, the passionate and almost demonic central character of Emily Bronte's romantic novel *Wuthering Heights*, was an orphan without pedigree.

Synonyms: descent, family tree, lineage, genealogy (jee nee AL uh jee)

Related words: progenitors, forebears, forefathers, heritage

6. *pittance* (PIT uns) *n.* small amount or portion, especially of money

Church sponsors in the Middle Ages sometimes donated money to a monastery to feast the monks on the successive anniversaries of the donor's death. This donation was a *pittance*, derived from Latin *pietas* ("piety," "devotion"). Originally a rather large and generous offering, the *pittance* dwindled until barely enough to provide crumbs for the monks. This shrunken *pittance* thus became synonymous with any small, inconsiderable, or inadequate amount.

Some people feel that Congress provides a pittance for education compared to the lavish expenditures for the military. Last year's high-priced fads can often be had today for a pittance. After losing their lucrative positions as a result of Senator Joseph McCarthy's witch hunt for Communists in the 1950's, several entertainers and screenwriters could find work that paid only a meager sum or pittance.

Synonyms: trifle, insufficiency, ration, minimal wage, modicum (MOD uh kum)

Related words: dole, meager remuneration

Contrasted words: abundance, largess, bounty

7. *preposterous* (prih POS tur us) *adj.*   ridiculous, obviously absurd, contrary to reason

From the ancient Romans we get the expression "to put the cart before the horse," meaning "to be mixed up" or "do things in the wrong order," since a horse normally pulls rather than pushes a cart. The Latin word conveying the sense of this expression was *praeposterus* (*pre* = "before," *post* = "after") and meant "having the last first," hence "not in the right way or manner." Therefore, our English word "presposterous" is truly a preposterous or absurd word since it literally derives from "before coming after." The Fool in Shakespeare's *King Lear* emphasizes the preposterousness of Lear's situation (King Lear had foolishly divided his kingdom between his two evil daughters while banishing his third devoted daughter) when he asks the king, "May not an ass know when the cart draws the horse?"— incidentally bringing to mind the etymology of "preposterous." It would be preposterous to kill a fly with a cannon. Someone preposterously proposed that an illiterate be chairman of the board of education.

Synonyms: foolish, nonsensical, silly, unreasonable, irrational, ludicrous
    (LOO dih krus)

Related words: fatuous, asinine, implausible, unfeasible

Contrasted words: plausible, credible, tenable, feasible

8. *macabre* (muh KAH bruh, muh KAHB) *adj.*   gruesome, horrible, causing fear, suggesting the horror of death

The Middle Ages produced morality plays in which abstract qualities like good deeds, poverty, wealth, and sin were represented by actors. These plays would teach a moral lesson through the conflict of good and evil to capture the souls of people. In one such morality play, Death debates with humans, wins the arguments, and leads the victims offstage in a weird *danse macabre* (French for "dance of death"). Medieval and Renaissance artists depicted the dance of death with Death in the form of a dancing skeleton. The Black Death, probably bubonic plague, wiped out approximately a third of Europe's population in the fourteenth century and contributed to the popularity of the gruesome *danse macabre* as a subject for art. With its horrid heritage of death, "macabre" most fittingly describes weird and terrifying events. Macabre films of horror and supernatural suspense often attract large audiences. Edgar Allan Poe and Stephen King are masters of the macabre.

Synonyms: grim, hideous, horrid, dreadful, weird, ghastly (GAST lee)

Related words: grisly, eerie, morbid

9. *farce* (FARS) *n.* ridiculous, light comedy; slapstick comedy; absurd thing; mockery

10. *bombast* (BOM bast) *n.* speech or writing that sounds grand or important but has little meaning

Both "farce" and "bombast" have to do with stuffing and padding. Since most people in the Middle Ages were illiterate, one way for them to learn about the Bible and religious events was through watching religious plays. However, the spectators sometimes grew restless as the actors took time out to change costumes between the acts of a play. Performers began to fill these gaps with light, humorous sketches called *farces*—from Latin *farcire* ("stuff")—since they were stuffed between acts. "Bombast" also derives from stuffing since men's court costumes in olden times were padded with cotton, this padding being called *bombace* in the French at that time. Today, lofty, flowery, high-sounding language lacking meaningful content is bombast, for it is essentially little more than padding. Bombastic speeches may even turn farcical if they become ridiculous enough. Intentional farces amuse us in T.V. situation comedies and films, but farces in justice where criminals go free are not amusing. In *Henry IV*, Shakespeare presents us with the swaggering, boasting, beer-bellied liar and joyful source of farcical entertainment— Falstaff, described by the hero, Price Hal, as "my sweet creature of bombast" (clearly alluding to Falstaff's padding, rolls of fat, and inflated speech).

Synonyms for "farce": mockery, absurdity, ridiculousness, nonsense, burlesque (bur LESK)

Related words for "farce": sham, travesty, parody, caricature

Synonyms for "bombast": wordiness, grandiloquence (gran DIL uh kwens)

Related words for "bombast": magniloquence, rhetoric, pretentiousness, pomposity

Working With Words

I. Fill in each blank with the appropriate word from the following list:

gadfly	pedigree
pittance	macabre
spurned	farce
Spartan	homage
preposterous	bombast

The life and teachings of the ancient Greek philosopher Socrates (469-399 B.C.) have made him one of history's most respected and influential figures. His lifestyle was simple, even (1)___Spartan___, eating plain food, wearing the same old robe throughout the year, and walking barefoot even on ice. However, he would occasionally party and could outdrink anyone on these occasions. Socrates' basic attitude to material comforts and luxuries can be seen when he looked at the numerous articles in a market place and remarked, "How many things there are that I do not want!" Whereas wealth meant nothing to Socrates, truth and goodness meant everything, the philosopher being credited with the saying "the unexamined life is not worth living." At that time there were teachers called "sophists," who, for a fee, would teach one how to win arguments. Socrates (2)___spurned___ the ways of these sophists, for he was concerned with discovering truth rather than winning debates and never accepted even a (3)___pittance___ for his teachings. Because he continually annoyed many of the citizens of Athens with his stinging inquiries into truth and justice, Socrates was known as the (4)___gadfly___ of Athens. His enemies brought him to trial with the charges of corruption of the youth and denial of traditional religion. In his defense, Socrates showed how wild, irrational, and (5)___preposterous___ were the charges of his accusers. Indeed, he made the opponents' arguments appear to be nothing but high-sounding speech with little meaning, mere (6)___bombast___. Socrates' skillful mockery of his prosecutors almost turned the trial into a ridiculous (7)___farce___. However, the majority of Athenians had made up their minds before the trial and condemned Socrates to death. In what may seem to us a (8)___macabre___ ending, although in reality it was a relatively gentle and peaceful death, Socrates drank the poison hemlock in his prison cell while surrounded by his weeping friends. His enemies succeeded in killing his body but not his thought. Western philosophy pays honor and (9) _____ *omage* to him by tracing its lineage or (10) _____ *pedigree* back to the ancient Greek philosophers, of whom Aristotle was a student of Plato and Plato a student of Socrates.

II. Match the word on the left with its synonyms.

_h_ 1. gadfly   a. reverence, respect

_f_ 2. farce   b. austere, severe

_d_ 3. pittance   c. repudiate, reject

_b_ 4. Spartan   d. modicum, trifle

_i_ 5. macabre   e. ludicrous, ridiculous

_j_ 6. pedigree   f. burlesque, mockery

_c_ 7. spurn   g. grandiloquence, wordiness

_a_ 8. homage   h. goad, critic

_g_ 9. bombast   i. ghastly, gruesome

_e_ 10. preposterous   j. genealogy, ancestry

III. Word Part: ROG—ask (surrogate)

prerogative (prih ROG uh tiv) *n.* exclusive or special right or privilege

derogatory (dih ROG uh tor ee) *adj.* tending to make a person or thing seem lower or of less value; belittling; negative; discrediting

interrogate (in TER uh gate) *v.* question formally, closely, systematically

arrogant (AR uh gunt) *adj.* showing an excessive and unpleasant sense of superiority; overbearingly proud; haughty

abrogate (AB ruh gate) *v.* abolish, repeal, cancel, legally do away with

Using each of the five ROG words only once, complete the following sentences.

1. I am not surprised that my political opponent makes negative, _derogatory_ remarks about my character.

2. Power and wealth transformed the humble, pleasant man into an _arrogant_ tyrant.

3. The Prohibition Era, the period when alcoholic beverages were illegal in the United States, began in 1920 and ended in 1933 when the government finally decided to _abrogate_ the Prohibition law.

4. It is the boss' _perogative_ to hire or fire anyone she wishes.

5. We will _interrogate_ the captured enemy officer about the number and location of his troops.

Chapter 3

1. *chimerical* (kuh MER ih kul) *adj.*   given to wildly impossible plans, unrealistic, fantastic, impractical

Fancy this—a fire-breathing monster with the head of a lion, the body of a goat, and the tail of a serpent—and you can picture the Greek mythological Chimera. This female monster devastated the land, shriveling crops and destroying herds of cattle and sheep. To the rescue came the hero Bellerophon astride his great winged horse Pegasus. Hovering on his mount beyond the belching flames of the Chimera, Bellerophon unerringly shot his arrows. Finally, he tipped his spear with a lump of lead, dove straight for the Chimera's gaping jaws, and forced the lead down her throat. The Chimera's own flames melted the lead so that the molten metal fatally burned her vital organs. Though the Chimera died, her name lives on for any plan or scheme as wildly fantastic and unrealistic as herself.

Many believed that the Wright brothers' plan for an airplane and Robert Fulton's idea for a steamboat were mere chimeras. However, success proved these men not to be chimerical dreamers but practical inventors who revolutionized society.

Synonyms: imaginary, fanciful, quixotic (kwik SOT ik)

Related words: utopian, illusory

Contrasted words: pragmatic, mundane

2. *asinine* (ASS uh nine) *adj.* stupid or silly

"Asinine" derives from Latin *asinus* for "ass," "donkey." Since donkeys have the reputation for being stupid and stubborn, "asinine" acquired the meaning of stupid like a donkey. Interestingly, in the Bible (Numbers 22: 21-33) there is a story of Balaam and his ass. Balaam was a magician and priest who saddled his female donkey and rode off to curse the Israelites. However, the Lord placed in their path an angel with a sword, ready to slay Balaam. The donkey saw the angel; Balaam did not. Three times the ass refused to cross the path blocked by the angel, and three times Balaam savagely struck her. When the poor ass suffered the third blow from Balaam's staff, "the Lord opened the mouth of the ass, and she said to Balaam, 'What have I done to you, that you have struck me these three times?' " Then the Lord revealed to Balaam the angel of death with drawn sword. Balaam immediately fell to his knees and asked forgiveness. Ironically, Balaam's initial actions were asinine while those of his ass were compassionately wise. "Balaam's ass" has become a symbol of natural, purely innocent devotion. Incidentally, the only other time an animal speaks in the Bible is when in the Garden of Eden the snake tempts Eve.

In Middle English, the language of Chaucer's time, there was one word *ars* for the posterior or buttocks, and another word *asse* for ass or donkey. However, speakers often tend to drop the letter "r," as can be observed in certain regions where "sir" is pronounced "suh" and "mister" pronounced "mistuh." In this way, *ars* came to be pronounced "ass." Since it was a taboo or forbidden word, the similarity of its sound to the "ass" meaning "donkey" made people also reluctant to use "ass" to refer to the animal. Today, therefore, we usually tend to avoid "ass" in either sense in polite society, but our ancestors who translated the Bible into English in Shakespeare's time had no such reservations for the King James Bible has made famous "Balaam's ass."

I lost my job when my supervisor told me not to ask any more asinine questions and I asininely responded, "Why not?"

Synonyms: foolish, mindless, idiotic, ridiculous, absurd, inane (ih NAYN, rhymes with "pain")

Related words: fatuous, puerile, ludicrous, crass

Contrasted words: sage, prudent, judicious

3. *bellwether* (BEL weth ur) *n.* leader

"Bellwether" is an old word in English referring to a castrated male sheep ("whether") that had a bell around its neck and would lead other sheep. Since people similarly tend to flock around a leader, a person in a leading position is also known as a bellwether. Susan B. Anthony became a bellwether in the movement to gain voting rights for women in the United States. Nashville, Tennessee, bellwether of country music, attracts a multitude of songwriters, singers, and musicians.

Synonyms: pacesetter, pacemaker, vanguard (VAN gard) ["vanguard" refers to leaders, leadership, or a leading position]

4. *limbo* (LIM bo) *n.* place or state of neglect; period awaiting change; in-between state

According to some Christian beliefs, the souls of unbaptized infants who have not sinned and of holy people who died before Christian times go to a place called limbo. "Limbo" derives from Latin *limbus* ("border") since it is a region that borders hell, but without hell's agonizing punishments. Perhaps the greatest literary portrayal of the afterlife is the Italian epic poem *The Divine Comedy* by Dante (1265-1321). In this work, Dante vividly traces the soul's journey from the torments of hell to the bliss of heaven. Dante imagined limbo as a region where worthy ancients such as the philosopher Socrates and the poet Homer (author of the *Iliad* and *Odyssey*) dwelled. Today, many people use "limbo," unaware of its religious derivation. For instance, they will say that they are in limbo while deciding what to do after having left one job before taking another. If we feel we are going nowhere, we are in a state of limbo. I always feel that I am in limbo when my telephone call is put on hold. Though still retaining its religious meaning, "limbo" commonly refers to states of neglect and transition in our everyday life.

Synonyms: neglect, transition, oblivion (uh BLIV ee un)

5. *plagiarize* (PLAY juh rize) *v.* use ideas or writings of another and present them as one's own

Don't get ensnared in a web of vice by passing another's work off as your own. Actually, the word "plagiarize"—which refers to this act of stealing—originates with snares, stealing, and vice. Ancient Romans called a sea raider or plunderer *plagiarus*, from Latin *plaga* ("net"), for these raiders seized booty and victims in their nets. Since they often stole and then sold children as slaves, *plagiarus* came to mean "kidnapper." Metaphorically, when we use someone else's work as our own or plagiarize, we are stealing that person's brainchild or thought. Of course, ideas about what constitutes plagiarism have differed throughout history. Shakespeare, who freely borrowed plots and ideas from others, might be considered a plagiarist according to a strict interpretation of plagiarism by today's standards; however, he was an honest writer according to the conventions of his time, and transformed the writings of others into his own unique unsurpassed drama with soaring language, unforgettable characters, and soul-searching conflict.

Synonyms: copy, steal, rob, purloin (pur LOYN) ["purloin" refers to stealing in general, not just of ideas or writings]

Related words: filch, pilfer

6. *titanic* (ty TAN ik) *adj.* enormous in size or strength

Before Zeus became the supreme ruler, Greek mythology recounts how the Titans—giants with incredible strength—lorded over the universe. Zeus overthrew the Titans, aided by one of the Titans themselves—Prometheus. However, Prometheus later angered Zeus by stealing fire from heaven and giving it to humans. For punishment, Zeus chained this benefactor of humanity to a rock and sent an eagle every day to feast upon Prometheus' liver, which would grow back every night. Centuries later the hero Hercules ended this torture by slaying the eagle and tearing open Prometheus' chains. Hercules, evidently, possessed even more titanic strength than the Titan, for Prometheus had been unable to break the chains. Some athletes, stricken by accident or disease, make titanic efforts to resume their careers and ultimately become world champions. Beethoven is a giant or titan in music, Rembrandt a titan in art, and Shakespeare a titan in literature. Twentieth-century American author Theodore Dreiser, best known for his novels *Sister Carrie* and *An American Tragedy*, also wrote a novel about a ruthless, enormously wealthy and influential business tycoon, aptly titled *The Titan*.

Synonyms: gigantic, huge, enormous, prodigious (pruh DIJ us)

Related words: colossal, gargantuan, mammoth

Contrasted words: diminutive, minuscule, minute (my NOOT), puny

7. *irony* (EYE ruh nee) *n.* expression that means the opposite of what is stated; event or result the opposite of what is expected.

The etymologist Joseph Shipley said, "Irony is a blow delivered as a caress, an insult presented as a compliment." Irony occurs when things are otherwise than they appear. The source of this word is from the Greek *eiron*, a traditional character in ancient Greek drama who feigned ignorance and used his tricks (*eironeia*) to outwit his bragging, conceited opponent. Similarly, the philosopher Socrates used a method of argument called Socratic irony in which he pretended ignorance in order to trap his audience into logical errors.

An ironic remark might be "Just wonderful" in answer to a question about how was your day—a day you ran out of gas in a thunderstorm, discovered that you had lost your wallet as you went to pay for lunch, and came home to find your new furniture torn apart by the children's puppy. Ironically, we no sooner attain our heart's desire than we quickly become dissatisfied and seek something else. Such is the irony of life. Closely related to irony is sarcasm—a ridiculing, bitter, scornful remark.

Synonyms: contradiction, mockery, sarcasm (SAR kaz um)

Related words: satire, cynicism, paradox

Contrasted words: bluntness, frankness, candor

8. *effete* (ih FEET) *adj.* worn-out, unproductive, barren

As mothers know, the term "labor" aptly describes the prolonged, wearying ordeal of childbirth. The ancient Romans acknowledged this arduous effort with their word *effetus* (*ef* [a variant of *ex*] = "out," *fetus* = "having produced" [young, offspring, children]) which came to mean "worn out by bearing," "exhausted." When the Latin word entered English as "effete," it was used to describe livestock worn-out by bearing offspring. "Effete" then extended its meaning to become a general term for "exhausted" and "lacking vitality, vigor, and energy." We now apply "effete" to anything worn-out, such as civilizations (some say the Roman Empire fell because its civilization had become effete), art styles (those who don't understand modern or abstract art often label it effete), and individuals (an effete person has lost his/her drive and productivity). Etymologically related to "effete" is "fetus"—the unborn child in the mother's womb.

Synonyms: unproductive, exhausted, feeble, decadent (DEK un dunt)

Related words: sterile, enervated, impotent, degenerate

Contrasted words: flourishing, prolific, fecund, vital

9. *hyperbole* (hy PUR buh lee) *n.* obviously extravagant statement or assertion

10. *diabolic* (dy uh BOL ik) *adj.* outrageously wicked; cruel; devilish

"The devil himself could not change that person's mind" is clearly a hyperbole or figure of speech unless the "person" is the umpire in the novel *The Year the Yankees Lost the Pennant* (later made into the musical *Damn Yankees*). In this work, the devil restores the youth of a middle-aged baseball fan who hates the New York Yankees. The rejuvenated fan acquires phenomenal baseball skills in exchange for his soul. However, at the end of the season, he gains back his soul and aging body as he rounds the bases attempting to score the pennant-winning run. As he slides into home, the umpire screams "Safe!" and even the devil himself cannot get the umpire to change his decision. "Hyperbole" derives from Greek *hyperbole* meaning "exaggeration" or "extravagance" (*hyper* = "beyond," "over," "excessive" + *bol* = "throw") since one overstates or throws words excessively. "He hit the ball a mile," "We have waited forever," and "I died laughing" are all common hyperboles. Etymologically related to "hyperbole" is "diabolic" from Greek *dia* ("across") + *bol* ("throw"). The Greek translation of the Hebrew *satan* ("adversary," "opponent") into *diabolos* ("slanderer") conveyed the idea of the devil throwing slimy lies across the path of his victim, in other words, a mudslinger; in addition, *diabolos* probably conveyed the idea of the devil throwing souls across to hell. Hollywood escape films often confront the hero with hyperbolic, exaggerated villains who fiendishly construct some devilishly evil, diabolic plan. The adjective "diabolic" has an alternate form "diabolical." It has been said that hyperbole lies without deceiving. Diabolically, the devil uses the literal truth to deceive according to the phrase "the devil can cite Scripture for his purpose" (from Shakespeare's *The Merchant of Venice*).

Synonyms for "hyperbole": overstatement, rhetorical (rih TOR ih kul) exaggeration

Related words for "hyperbole": embellishment, amplification

Contrasted words for "hyperbole": understatement, litotes

Synonyms for "diabolic": evil, fiendish, demonic, satanic, infernal (in FUR nul)

Related words for "diabolic": nefarious, execrable, heinous, iniquitous, impious, Mephistophelian

Contrasted words for "diabolical": pious, virtuous, benevolent, humane

Working With Words

I. Fill in each blank with the appropriate word from the following list:

chimerical	bellwether
limbo	diabolically
plagiarizing	titanic
ironically	asinine
hyperbole	effete

An outstanding football, basketball, and baseball player, Adam Budd was not only the leading sports figure at Arcadia College but also a (1)___bellwether___ in the academic life—captain of the debating team, editor of the college newspaper, and most likely candidate for valedictorian. Both fellow students and teachers were given to (2)___hyperbole___ in describing his achievements. The focus of this exaggerated praise was of average height and weight, but his deceptive appearance housed (3)___titanic___ strength (he could lift one end of a car above his head and actually bend prison bars with his bare hands). He could also perform startling mental feats with his photographic memory and computer-like calculations. One student at Arcadia College, however, bitterly resented Adam's colossal achievements—rich, lazy, spoiled Nick Claggert. Though he once had tremendous potential, Nick had squandered his energies with gambling, drinking, and other decadent pursuits so that he had become worn-out and (4)___effete___, incapable of being intellectually or academically productive. Bitterly envious, Nick conceived the fanciful, (5)___chimerical___ plan of (6)___plagiarizing___ Adam's senior honor's thesis and presenting it as his own. Though the plan might appear stupid and (7)___asinine___—Adam's writing style and level of achievement were so obviously different from Nick's—the (8)___diabolically___ clever Nick somehow managed to convince Adam's girlfriend that Adam and he were coauthors of a project. She then returned with Adam's research and helped Nick revise the work. However, Adam had recently decided to discard his project, for he discovered that a scholar at a major university had done almost exactly the same project. With phenomenal speed, Adam conceived, researched, and completed his new thesis which won highest honors. One of Arcadia college's professors, however, was a close friend of the scholar whose project resembled the one Adam had discarded. This Arcadia professor brought charges of plagiarism against Nick. Currently Nick is in a state of (9)_____*limbo*_____, not knowing yet whether he will ever graduate or be expelled. The accusing professor cannot find any wording in the plagiarized paper closely resembling that of the university scholar. (10)_____*Normally*_____, the Arcadia professor would have accepted the similarity of the two papers as coincidental if an outstanding student like Adam Budd was involved, but the professor can only believe that a decadent student like Nick Claggert must have plagiarized.

II. Match the word on the left with its synonyms.

____1. plagiarize   a. inane, foolish

____2. limbo   b. quixotic, fantastic

____3. effete   c. prodigious, gigantic

____4. diabolic   d. oblivion, transition

____5. titanic   e. vanguard, leader

____6. asinine   f. decadent, exhausted

____7. hyperbole   g. sarcasm, mockery

____8. chimerical   h. purloin, steal

____9. bellwether   i. infernal, fiendish

___10. irony   j. rhetorical exaggeration, overstatement

III. Word Part: DUR—hard, lasting (during, endurance)

durable (DOOR uh bul) *adj.* lasting a long time; resisting wear and decay

endure (in DOOR) *v.* exist, last; bear, put up with patiently

duration (doo RAY shun) *n.* time something lasts or continues

duress (doo RES) *n.* force or threats to make someone do something

obdurate (OB doo rut) *adj.* stubborn, unyielding, hardhearted

Using each of the five DUR words only once, complete the following sentences.

1. With a gun pointed at his head, the victim declared that he was signing the contract under ____duress____.

2. We could not persuade the ____obdurate____ father to change his mind and allow his son to join the community center.

3. Do you think you could ____endure____ the winters of Alaska after growing up in Florida?

4. Perishable goods spoil rapidly; ____durable____ goods last a long time.

5. For her sin of adultery, Hester Prynne wore the scarlet letter "A" on her bosom for the ____duration____ of her life.

Chapter 4

1. *dunce* (DUNS) *n.* stupid person

One of the most brilliant men of his time, the philosopher John Duns Scotus (1265-1308) has provided us with a word for poor learners and blockheads. Duns Scotus challenged the ideas of another philosopher of his period, the great St. Thomas Aquinas (1225-1274), a major influence on Christian, particularly Roman Catholic, thought. In turn, Aquinas' followers attacked the positions of Duns Scotus and his students, known as *Duns men*. Perhaps these attacks helped to give the *Duns men* a bad name. But most authorities believe that it was the picky, hairsplitting, absurdly subtle reasoning of the *Duns men* over the next two centuries that made them ridiculed by the new thinkers of the Renaissance and branded the *Duns men* as stupid opponents of progressive thought. Hence, because of his petty, narrow-minded disciples—called *Duns men*, *Dunses*, and eventually *Dunces*—the name of the intellectual giant Duns Scotus has become associated with stupidity.

To add insult to injury, a tall cone-shaped paper hat called a fool's cap or dunce cap was placed on the head of outstandingly bad students in times past. The hat most likely got its name from "foolscap"—a type of paper approximately 13 x 16 inches with the faint distinguishing mark of a fool's cap and bells (the costume of the old court jester). However, because the dunces in the class wore this hat, the hat became known as a dunce cap, ironically further degrading the good name of the master teacher Duns Scotus.

Synonyms: blockhead, simpleton, fool, dolt (rhymes with "colt")

Related words: ignoramus, dullard

Contrasted words: sage, savant, pundit, prodigy

2. *charlatan* (SHAR luh tun) *n.* deceiver who falsely claims to have knowledge or skill; impostor

Just as Sicily has an unfortunate association with the Mafia, so did the Italian village of Cerreto become known for its cheats. The villagers were said to babble (*ciarlare* in Italian) deceptively, giving rise to Italian *ciarlatano* ("babbler," "phony")—*ciarlatano* being an altered form of *cerretano*, "an inhabitant of Cerreto"—from which our word "charlatan" derives, entering the English language in the seventeenth century. There is a story that in the nineteenth century a famous quack dentist, A. M. Latan, toured Paris. At his approach, spectators would shout "Voilà le char de Latan" ("There is Latin's car"). Presumably, the words "char de latan" associated with this fake reinforced the meaning of "charlatan."

Another word of Italian origin—"mountebank"—is almost an exact synonym for "charlatan." Quacks and impostors in medieval Italy would go to the public square and, often accompanied by a juggler or other entertainer to attract a crowd, mount (*monta*) a bench (*banco*) and proceed to sell the crowd worthless goods. The traveling salesman in cowboy movies who sells snake oil to "cure whatever ails you" is another version of a mountebank or charlatan.

Hans Christian Anderson wrote "The Emperor's New Clothes" about a king who commissioned two weavers to make him the finest clothes of gold, silver, and silk. The weavers assured the king that the clothes were magical, for the garments were invisible to fools. Of course, the weavers were swindlers who kept the gold, silver, and silk for themselves and only went through the motions of spinning and weaving nonexistent thread. Afraid to be discovered a fool, everyone at court praised the emperor's new clothes although no one saw anything. Unable to admit he was a fool, the emperor stripped to put on the new clothes. He then marched in a grand procession to display his garments to the public. Since word had spread about the magical nature of the clothes, everyone pretended to see splendid royal attire. Everyone except a little boy. The innocent child shouted, "The emperor is naked!" Instantly, the crowd broke into an acknowledging roar. Embarrassingly confronted with the naked truth, the emperor realized he had been duped by the two charlatans or mountebanks.

In Mark Twain's *Huckleberry Finn*, Huck and Jim have numerous adventures with the charlatans the Duke and the Dauphin, two of the most hilarious mountebanks in literature. Hopefully, we will avoid charlatans and mountebanks when we look for a car, house, or investments.

Synonyms: swindler, quack, cheat, mountebank (MOUNT uh bank)

Related words: fraud, confidence man

3. *sycophant* (SIK uh funt) *n.* sickeningly humble self- seeking flatterer

Strange as it seems, etymologists trace the repulsive word "sycophant" to a seemingly harmless fruit—the fig. For some, "sycophant"—from Greek *sykon* ("fig") + *phainen* ("show")—goes back to ancient Greek smugglers of figs. Supposedly, informers used the "sign of the fig" (a clenching of the fist with the thumb sticking between two fingers) to accuse smugglers before a judge. Because the informers hoped to gain the favor of the judge, *sykophantes* ("one who makes the 'sign of the fig' ") became associated with insincere, self-seeking flattery. Other etymologists, however, remind us that the "sign of the fig" was (and still is in the Mediterranean area) an obscene gesture similar in meaning to a finger gesture used today. They conclude that the meaning of this gesture aptly conveyed the loathing felt for nauseating, insincere flatterers. In what many consider the greatest work of the Middle Ages— *The Divine Comedy*—the Italian poet Dante employs the "sign of the fig" to show the utter lack of repentance of a soul damned in hell:

> When he had finished saying this, the thief
> shaped his fists into figs and raised them high
> and cried: "Here, God, I've shaped them just for you!"

"Toady," another name for a sycophant, derives from the swindling traveling medicine man of past centuries. An assistant accompanied this charlatan or fraud. The assistant would eat (or pretend to eat) a presumably poisonous toad. The mountebank or fake doctor would then produce an antidote to the poison which the assistant swallowed. When the crowd saw the assistant cured, the charlatan would then sell his potion. Because of his taste for toads, the assistant acquired the name of "toady." His disgusting manner of serving the fraudulent doctor caused his name to pass into our language as an equally loathsome substitute for "sycophant."

People suffering misfortune learn that "a friend in need is a friend indeed"; people newly acquiring a fortune may find themselves surrounded by false friends, sycophants, and toadies. Colloquially, an "Uncle Tom" refers to a sycophant or toady.

Synonyms: flatterer, flunky, toady (TOH dee)

Related words: groveler, fawner, lackey, truckler, kowtower, parasite

4. *anachronism* (uh NAK ruh nizm) *n.* something out of its proper historical time; error of putting something in the wrong historical time

English teachers love to point out that the striking of the clocks in Shakespeare's *Julius Caesar* is an anachronism since not until over a thousand years after Caesar's assassination were striking clocks invented. Another famous anachronism is the story of the youthful George Washington's throwing a silver dollar across the Potomac River; silver dollars were not minted until after Washington had become President. "Anachronism" derives from Greek *ana* ("back," "backward") + *chronos* ("time"), referring to something "back-timed" or "out of time," hence the assigning of something to the wrong period.

Set in his old ways, my father is a dinosaur of fashion, a walking anachronism. Caps and gowns at graduation are anachronistic attire, reminders of the garments of the monks who kept learning alive during the Middle Ages.

Synonyms: time error, chronological (kron uh LOJ ik kul) error

5. *draconian* (dray KOH nee un) *adj.* severe, harsh, cruel

Can you imagine a system of law where almost every crime—even stealing a cabbage—is punishable by death? Such was the legal system codified in 621 B.C. by the Greek Athenian statesman Draco. Draco, however, merely systematized and gave written form to Athens' unwritten laws already in effect. In fact, the publication of the Draconian Code replaced private revenge with public justice and prevented judges from openly favoring the upper classes. So harsh were the laws, however, that it came to be said that Draco's laws were written in blood. Thirty years later, the great Athenian lawmaker Solon modified the laws, keeping the death penalty only for murder. For the laws that he recorded but did not originate, Draco has become immortalized in "draconian," referring to extremely harsh rules, laws, and methods.

The chairman argued that only short-term draconian measures of slashing salaries in half, eliminating paid vacations, and canceling insurance policies could prevent bankruptcy. Accustomed as we are to our own system of law, we may shudder at societies that inflict the draconian punishment of chopping off the offending hand of a shoplifter.

Synonyms: strict, stern, rigorous, austere (aw STEER)

Related words: stringent, despotic

Contrasted words: lenient, indulgent, tolerant

6. *plummet* (PLUM it) *v.* fall rapidly straight down

Ever wonder why the symbol for lead is Pb? Pb is the abbreviation for *plumbum*, Latin for "lead." Plumbers got their name from working with lead pipes. In days before sonar, sailors used to measure the depths of the waters with a plumb line or plummet—a string at whose end was a lead weight. The seaman who took the reading was a "leadsman" (from the lead at the end of the line). The author of *Huckleberry Finn* and *Tom Sawyer* referred to this procedure in explaining the origin of his pseudonym or pen name: "I want to sign my articles …'Mark Twain.' It is an old river term, a leads-man's call, signifying two fathoms—twelve feet." Because a plumb line or plummet falls straight down (carpenters also use this instrument to determine a 90 degree angle), "plummet" came to be used as a verb meaning to "plunge," "drop straight down."

When stock market prices plummet or drop sharply, investors panic. That strange visitor from another planet—Superman—came here as a baby when the rocket carrying him plummeted to Earth.

Synonyms: plunge, drop, fall, dive, descend, hurtle (HUR tul) ["move or throw with great speed," not necessarily downward]

Contrasted words: ascend, soar

7. *fatal* (FAY tul) *adj.* causing or capable of causing death and destruction

8. *nefarious* (nih FARE ee us) *adj.* extremely wicked

"Whatever will be will be." The concept goes back to the Fates of Greek and Roman mythology, three goddesses who spun, measured out, and cut the thread of life—thus determining when a person would live and die. Nothing could alter the fate or destiny they wove. Well, almost nothing. On rare occasions, such as that involving King Admetus—a friend of Hercules, the mightiest of Greek heroes—the Fates could be persuaded. Shortly before King Admetus' thread of life was to be snipped, the Fates agreed to postpone his death if the king could find someone to take his place. Much to his surprise, Admetus found no one, not even his mother, father, or closest friend, willing to die for him. Finally, his wife Alcestis offered to sacrifice herself so that he might live. When Hercules visited his friend Admetus, the mighty hero found the house in mourning for the queen. However, Alcestis was too good a host to make Hercules aware of this event and merely told Hercules that some woman in the household, but no relative, had died. Believing that no great tragedy had occurred, Hercules proceeded to his room and became roaring drunk. He felt offended, however, when no servants would join his riotous festivity. Fastening his superhuman grip on a servant, Hercules managed to extract the real reason for the household's sorrow. Instantly shamed, Hercules decided to make up for his unseemly behavior by going down to Hades (the realm of the dead) and wrestling Death for possession of Alcestis. Victorious, Hercules restored the queen to life and to her husband. On almost no other occasion, however, could one alter the deadly decision of the Fates. Hence, "fatal" came to have its meaning of "deadly." Also from the same source derives "fatality" ("disastrous death"), "fatalism" ("belief that everything is determined and that therefore nothing can be done to change it"), and "fatalist" ("person who believes that all events are fixed beforehand and therefore no one can change them"). Just as "fate" derives from Latin *fari* ("speak") and *fatum* ("prophetic speaking of the gods"), so "nefarious" (from *ne* = "not," *fari* = "speak") meant "unholy," "offensive to the gods," referring to the outrageous or unspeakable. English "nefarious" retains the intensely negative meaning of "extremely wicked, evil."

In Shakespeare's *Macbeth*, there are three "weird sisters" who prophesy Macbeth's future. Earlier, in the Middle English of Chaucer's time, the three Fates were known as the "weird sisters." Thus, Shakespeare's three witches or "weird sisters" still retain the idea of involvement in fate or destiny. Some regard these witches as nefariously trapping Macbeth; others consider Macbeth's fatal outcome the result of his own nefarious actions.

Synonyms for "fatal": deadly, ruinous, disastrous, destructive, lethal (LEE thal)

Related words for "fatal": mortal, pernicious, terminal

Contrasted words for "fatal": auspicious, propitious, benign, innocuous, vitalizing, restorative

Synonyms for "nefarious": wicked, evil, heinous (HAY nus)

Related words for "nefarious": vile, infamous, abominable, odious, atrocious, iniquitous, execrable, opprobrious, flagrant

Contrasted words for "nefarious": laudable, virtuous, exalted

9. *vindicate* (VIN duh kate) *v.* clear from blame, charges, criticism; justify

10. *vindictive* (vin DIK tive) *adj.* revengeful

Both "vindicate" and "vindictive" stem from Latin *vindicare* ("revenge," "defend," "set free"). One way of settling disputes in ancient Rome was for two contestants to take rods and cross them as if to fight. The judge would then render his decision, and the winner would proceed to break the loser's rod or *vindiciae*. Hence, the victorious party was vindicated or set free from charges. Of course, the defeated contestant might still harbor feelings of vindictiveness or revenge.

In a famous court case at the end of the nineteenth century, the French army officer Alfred Dreyfus was court-martialed for treason and sentenced to life imprisonment on Devil's Island. Sensing injustice, the French novelist Émile Zola championed Dreyfus' cause, eventually resulting in a retrial vindicating Dreyfus by showing him to be the innocent victim of a plot. In another famous military trial, the U.S. Army general Billy Mitchell was found guilty in 1915 for defying his superiors because of his intense beliefs in the importance of air power as a military force. World War II vindicated Mitchell's air-power theories, showing them to be correct. The words of Abraham Lincoln are applicable to the cases of Dreyfus and Mitchell: "Truth is generally the best vindication against slander." Two of literature's most vindictive characters are Captain Ahab (fanatic pursuer of the white whale Moby Dick who chewed off his leg) and Edmund Dantes, better known as the Count of Monte Cristo.

Synonyms for "vindicate": justify, clear, uphold, absolve (ab ZOLV)

Related words for "vindicate": exonerate, exculpate, substantiate, corroborate, verify

Contrasted words for "vindicate": refute, censure, castigate, rebuke, reproach

Synonyms for "vindictive": spiteful, unforgiving, vengeful (VENJ ful)

Related words for "vindictive": avenging, retaliatory, retaliative

Working With Words

I. Fill in each blank with the appropriate word from the following list:

dunce	draconian
charlatan	nefarious
vindictive	anachronism
sycophant	vindicate
plummeted	fatal

Each word must be used only once.

The Book of Esther in the Old Testament recounts that King Ahasuerus of Persia made the beautiful Jewish woman Esther his queen. Mordecai, a cousin of Esther's, told Esther not to reveal her religion to the king. Shortly after Esther's marriage, the king made a man called Haman his top official. Everyone was ordered to bow down before Haman, but Mordecai refused. Haman—a most (1)__*vindictive*__ or revengeful character—determined to take severely harsh or (2)__*draconian*__ action against Mordecai and the Jews. Haman convinced the king to decree the death of all the Jews—every man, woman, and child. Mordecai learned of this wicked, (3)__*nefarious*__ plot and asked Esther for help. Esther was no (4)__*dunce*__; she had brains as well as beauty. Inviting Haman to a dinner with her and the king, Esther revealed herself as a Jew and managed to (5)__*vindicate*__ her people to King Ahasuerus. She exposed the nefarious Haman for what he truly was—a self-seeking, flattering (6)__*sycophant*__ who promoted his own interest at the expense of the kingdom. Haman's fortunes (7)__*plummeted*__ sharply. King Ahasuerus no longer looked upon Haman as a genuine, reliable advisor but as a grasping, deceiving (8)__*charlatan*__. The king hanged Haman on the very gallows Haman had prepared for Mordecai. Haman's vindictive plot proved his own (9)__*fatal*__ undoing. Jewish people retell this story every year during the festival of Purim. To say that Abraham and Moses celebrated Purim would be an (10)__*anachronism*__, however, for these men lived long before the events described in the Book of Esther.

II. Match the word on the left with its synonyms.

_b_ 1. vindicate   a. lethal, deadly

_c_ 2. plummet   b. absolve, justify

_d_ 3. charlatan   c. hurtle, plunge

_i_ 4. draconian   d. mountebank, swindler

_a_ 5. fatal   e. toady, flatterer

_g_ 6. vindictive   f. dolt, fool

_e_ 7. sycophant   g. vengeful, unforgiving

_h_ 8. nefarious   h. austere, severe

_j_ 9. anachronism   i. heinous, evil

_f_ 10. dunce   j. chronological error, time error

III. Word Part: DICT—speak, say (predict, contradict)

indict (in DYT) *v.* accuse of a crime, especially to put a subject on trial after being accused of a crime

malediction (mal uh DIK shun) *n.* curse

diction (DIK shun) *n.* style or choice of words, especially in regard to pronunciation

edict (EE dikt) *n.* public command or order by one in high authority; decree

jurisdiction (joor iss DIK shun) *n.* legal authority, especially in regard to its range or extent

Using each of the five DICT words only once, complete the following sentences.

1. According to a city ____edict____, all businesses have to close by midnight.

2. The English guest speaker impressed the audience with his fine ____diction____.

3. United States law enforcers do not have ____jurisdiction____ over criminals who flee to other countries.

4. The drug lord feared the grand jury might ____indict____ him.

5. The evil sorcerer threatened to put a ____malediction____ on the kingdom.

Chapter 5

1. venerate	6. vegetate
2. sadistic	7. adamant
3. malapropism	8. conjugal
4. pragmatic	9. abominable
5. disparage	10. ominous

1. *venerate* (VEN uh rate) *v.* regard with great respect

Etymology makes strange bedfellows. Linguistically, the wild, uninhibited, eternally youthful love goddess Venus is the mother of venerable (greatly respected or honored) old men. "Venerable" derives from Latin *venerari* ("worship," "seek a god's favor"), which in turn comes from *venus* ("love"), Venus being the personification of love or desire. In an ancient Roman myth, the sculptor Pygmalion, scorning women as flawed creatures, made a statue embodying his ideal of a perfect woman. Falling hopelessly in love with his sculpture, Pygmalion went to Venus' temple to pray that he could meet a girl resembling the statue. Upon returning home, Pygmalion could not resist embracing and kissing his creation. Miraculously, he felt his kiss and embrace returned. Because he had venerated Venus, the goddess granted his wish by transforming the statue into a real woman, henceforth called Galatea. George Bernard Shaw incorporated this myth in his play *Pygmalion*, which in turn inspired the musical *My Fair Lady*. Although we may no longer venerate the deities of classical mythology, we still indirectly honor Venus when we use the words "venerable" and "venerate."

Synonyms: respect, honor, admire, worship, revere (rih VEER)

Related words: idolize, esteem, extol

Contrasted words: spurn, deride, execrate

2. *sadistic* (suh DIS tik) *adj.* getting pleasure from hurting others

The Marquis de Sade (1740-1814) was 5 feet two and some say his eyes were blue, but whatever color his eyes were, his slight, handsome body housed a viciously cruel soul. The French nobleman delighted in torturing his sexual victims—from prostitute to wife. In retaliation for his cruelty to her daughter, his mother-in-law succeeded in getting the courts to sentence him with the death penalty. De Sade fled but spent much of his remaining life in prison or the insane asylum. Because of his unnatural delight in inflicting pain on others (amply described in his novels and other works), de Sade has spawned the words "sadism," "sadist," and "sadistic." Whereas a sadist loves to give pain to others, a masochist (MAS uh kust) takes pleasure in receiving pain. The Austrian novelist Leopold von Sacher-Masoch (1835-95)—from whom "masochist" derives—enjoyed being lashed with studded whips and being betrayed by his lovers. Like the two ends of a magnet, sadism and masochism are polar opposites whose practitioners attract each other. If a sadist were to address a masochist, "Watch out or I will hurt you," a likely reply might be, "Do it, do it."

Horror stories abound about the brutal, sadistic torture of presumed witches in the Middle Ages. Some perfectionists are almost masochistically obsessive in the mental and emotional anguish they undergo to achieve their goals.

Synonyms: brutal, vicious, perversely (pur VURS lee) cruel

Related words: fiendish, perverted

Contrasted words: masochistic

3. *malapropism* (MAL uh prop iz um) *n.* ridiculous or humorous misuse of words

Imagine a President saying, "We must lend a helping hand to our urine friends"—certainly a gross and ridiculous blunder of the word "urine" for "European" (the author actually heard the mixing up of these words in a Presidential broadcast). Such a ridiculous confusion of words is a malapropism. "Malapropism" derives from the character Mrs. Malaprop in *The Rivals* (1775) by the Irish-English playwright Richard Sheridan. Mrs. Malaprop spouted such gems as "Illiterate [for 'obliterate'] him, I say, quite from your memory" and "She might reprehend [for 'comprehend'] the true meaning of what she was saying." From Mrs. Malaprop—aptly named from the French *mal* ("badly") and *a propos* ("to the purpose," "appropriately") to signify something not to the purpose or unfitting and not appropriate—comes the word "malapropism." Almost two hundred years before *The Rivals*, Shakespeare used malapropisms in his comic creations. For example, in *Measure for Measure* the law officer Elbow humorously abuses his wife while intending to defend her honor: "My wife, sir, whom I detest [for 'protest'] before heaven … is an honest woman." Closely related to "malapropism" is "spoonerism"— "the accidental and humorous inter-changing of the initial sounds of words." The English Reverend William Spooner (1844 1930) was famous for such utterances. Presumably, he once lectured an audience on the "half-warmed fish inside me" (meaning to say the "half-formed wish") and referred to Queen Victoria as "our queer old dean" instead of "our dear old queen." During an oral literature examination, a nervous student named "Sheats and Kelley" as Romantic poets instead of Keats and Shelley. He stumbled from this spoonerism to a malapropism when he further referred to Regan and Goneril—the two evil daughters in Shakespeare's *King Lear*—as "Regan and Gonorrhea."

Synonyms: misusage, verbal blunder, spoonerism (SPOO nuh riz um)

Related words: solecism

4. *pragmatic* (prag MAT ik) *adj.* practical

Mention the James brothers and most people think of the outlaws Frank
and Jessie James. Born about the same time as the notorious bank
robbers, fellow Americans Henry (1843-1916) and William James
(1842-1910) became outstanding figures in the world of literature and
ideas. Henry James wrote complex, subtle, psychological novels and
short stories, the ghostly tale "The Turn of the Screw" being perhaps
the most famous. His brother William James helped develop the
philosophy of pragmatism and also made outstanding contributions to
psychology. Simply put, pragmatism states that the truth of an idea can
only be determined by its practical results. This philosophical doctrine
contributed to the everyday usage of "pragmatic" in the sense of "practical" and "sensible." In nineteenth-century England, the philosopher
John Stuart Mill became the leader of the utilitarian movement, which
asserted that public action should be determined by what does the most
good for the greatest number of people. Of course, Mill knew that
individuals have different ideas about what is good. Some prefer beer,
others Beethoven. In answer to criticism that he was advocating the
accumulation of gross pleasures, Mill retorted, "It is better to be
Socrates dissatisfied than a pig satisfied." This great philosopher also
staunchly supported the right of the minority to express its viewpoint:

> If all mankind minus one, were of one opinion, and
> only one person were of the contrary opinion,
> mankind would be no more justified in silencing that
> one person, than he, if he had the power, would be
> justified in silencing mankind.

Philosopher, political economist, and fighter for women's rights, Mill
popularized utilitarianism, resulting in "utilitarian" assuming the common, untechnical meaning of "useful," "practical," and "pragmatic."
Both "pragmatic" and "utilitarian" refer to the emphasis on usefulness
rather than on abstract qualities like truth, beauty, and goodness.

A rigid, theoretical administrator will not swerve from his master
plan, whereas a more pragmatic or utilitarian administrator will bend,
adjust, or compromise to get something accomplished. When the twentieth-century American author Langston Hughes announced his wish

to be a writer, his father pragmatically asked if Langston would make any money.

Synonyms: realistic, sensible, workable, utilitarian (yoo til uh TAIR [rhymes with "fair"] ee un)

Contrasted words: idealistic, speculative, theoretical, abstract

5. *disparage* (dis PAR ij) *v.* refer to something as having little importance; speak slightingly of

Derived from Latin *dis* ("away," "apart") and *parage* ("rank," "lineage"), "disparage" originally meant to "degrade socially by marrying beneath one's rank." "Disparage" then acquired the general meaning of "degrade," "undervalue," or "treat something as less than it is." In Grimm's fairy tale "King Thrushbeard," a spoiled, pampered princess speaks disparagingly of all her suitors. She particularly ridicules a handsome king by calling him "King Thrushbeard," for his pointed chin reminds her of the beak of a thrush (a songbird). Incensed at her treatment of the suitors, her father declares that she will marry the next beggar who comes to the palace. Shortly afterwards a poor musician enters. Steeling his heart against the hysterical protests of his daughter, the father marries her to the musician. Etymologically speaking, this is indeed a disparaging marriage for the princess since she has married far beneath her rank. The musician then schools her to humbleness as she learns to survive in poverty. Finally, the musician gets her a job as a kitchenmaid in the magnificent palace of King Thrushbeard. On one occasion she accidentally breaks some jars and flees in shame from the palace, only to be overtaken by King Thrushbeard himself—who reveals himself to be her disguised musician husband. Having learned humility, the princess now beams at her royal husband, no longer disparages marriage, and lives happily ever after. Before we make any disparaging remarks about the simplicity of fairy tales, let us gaze inward to see whether the haughty princess is not part of ourselves. Francis Bacon— English philosopher, statesman, and contemporary of Shakespeare— commented disparagingly of marriage: "He that hath a wife and children hath given hostages to fortune."

Synonyms: degrade, minimize, downgrade, belittle (bih LIT ul)

Related words: depreciate, deprecate, decry, denigrate, demean, detract

Contrasted words: laud, extol, commend, esteem

6. *vegetate* (VEJ uh tate) *v.* lead a dull, inactive, useless life

Left standing too long, vegetables become stale. Perhaps something like this process has happened to the word "vegetate." Originally, "vegetate" applied to the growth of plants and then to growth and development in general. This meaning logically stems from Latin *vegetare* ("grow," "enliven," "flourish"). We can even see the word "vegetable" used as an adjective descriptive of the life force for growth in Andrew Marvel's seventeenth-century seduction poem "To His Coy Mistress." Addressing his mistress, the narrator says:

> My vegetable love should grow
> Vaster than empires and more slow.

"Vegetable" here emphasizes growth, not slowness. However, as "vegetate" became part of the evolving stew of our language, its meaning changed to "be sluggish, or have little mental or physical activity." Vegetarians—people who do not eat animal products—may find the evolution of "vegetate" from its active to passive sense not to their taste.

Because he did not want to vegetate after retiring, my father did much volunteer work for the community.

Synonyms: be idle, be sluggish, stagnate (STAG nate)

Related words: languish, rusticate, be inert, be passive

7. *adamant* (AD uh munt) *adj.* unyielding, inflexible, definite

An adamant refusal is a firm refusal, as hard and unyielding as a rock. Fittingly, "adamant" derives from *adamas*, the Greek and Latin word for the hardest substances, whether real or imaginary. Although *adamas* was also the Greek word for "unbreakable," we can break *adamas* down to *a* ("not") and *damas* ("tame," "subdue," "breakdown," "marry"—

evidently, from the Greek point of view to marry a woman was somewhat analogous to taming an animal or subduing an enemy). Originally *adamas* meant any extremely hard metal or mineral, including diamonds; but in Late Latin (A.D. 200-600) *diamos* (a variant of *adamas*) began to be used solely for diamonds, the hardest of all substances found in nature. "Diamond" and "adamant" are thus linguistic relatives.

Baseball umpires adamantly refuse to change their decisions. Believers in the saying "If at first you don't succeed, try, try, again" are adamant in their conviction that perseverance breeds success.

Synonyms: firm, rigid, immovable, fixed, unchangeable, obdurate (OB du rut)

Related words: inexorable

Contrasted words: compliant, accommodating, capitulating

8. *conjugal* (KON juh gul) *adj.* of marriage; pertaining to the relationship between husband and wife

"Yoga" ("an Indian physical and spiritual discipline"), "conjugal" ("of marriage"), and "subjugate" ("conquer," "bring under control," "subdue")—what do these words have in common? All of them derive from the root *yug* ("join") from Indo-European, an ancient language that is the source of Sanskrit, Latin, Greek, English, and several other languages. The Indian word "yoga" from Sanskrit refers to a joining or union of the individual soul with the Infinite, Absolute, or in Western terms, God. "Yoga" also implies that we yoke (both "yoke" and "yoga" derive from *yug*) ourselves to a discipline to achieve spiritual union. Although most of us associate yoga with exaggerated twisting and stretching exercises, originally these exercises were preliminary to spiritual practices. "Subjugate" stems from Latin *sub* ("under") and *jugum* ("yoke"), for in ancient times conquered enemies had literally to crawl under three crossed spears similar in form to the yoke that subjugates oxen. Finally, "conjugal" comes from the prefix *con* ("with") accompanying the root for "yoke," implying that couples are joined or yoked together. Let us hope that when couples tie the conjugal knot, they also strive toward spiritual union and that one partner does not subjugate and make a defeated enemy or beast of burden of the other.

Synonyms: married, matrimonial, wedded, marital (MAR uh tul)

Related words: nuptial, connubial

9. *abominable* (uh BOM uh nuh bul) *adj.* utterly disgusting or hateful

10. *ominous* (OM uh nus) *adj.* threatening; suggestive of future evil

The ancient Greeks and Romans strongly believed that the gods sent signs or omens to predict good or evil in the future. In the *Iliad*, when the Greeks left a huge wooden horse secretly harboring their fiercest warriors before the gates of Troy, the Trojan priest Laocoön warned his countrymen not to admit this horse: "I fear the Greeks even when they bear gifts." Poseidon, god of the seas and friendly to the Greeks, then sent two huge serpents to wrap their fatal coils around Laocoön and his two sons. The Trojans mistook this event as an omen meaning the giant horse would be a blessing and admitted it to their city. The Trojan horse was their curse, for at night the Greek warriors came out and destroyed the city. English "omen" is a direct borrowing from Latin *omen*. The ancients would turn "away" (*ab*) in dread from an evil omen, the source of our words "abominate," "abomination," and "abominable." We turn away from something we abominate or hate, from abominations which are objects of disgust and hatred, and from that which is abominable or utterly offensive. Whereas an omen can be a positive or negative sign, "ominous"—which also derives from *omen*—solely refers to the negative. Ominous skies might mean a threatening thunderstorm, and a student who is cheating might catch an ominous glance from the teacher, signifying trouble ahead. Rumors abound that high in the Himalayas, a mountain range between India and Tibet, dwells the "abominable snowman," a monstrous, hairy, manlike creature. Unfortunately for the abominable snowman, his discovery by humans may be an ominous occasion that will lead to his extinction.

Synonyms for "abominable": revolting, horrible, awful, loathsome
(LOTH [rhymes with "both"] sum)

Related words for "abominable": abhorrent, detestable, despicable, horrid, repugnant, vile, odious, atrocious, execrable

Contrasted words for "abominable": laudable, commendable

Synonyms for "ominous": unfavorable, unlucky, sinister, menacing, ill-omened, foreboding (for BOH ding)

Related words for "ominous": dire, direful, baleful, inauspicious, unpropitious

Contrasted words for "ominous": auspicious, benign, propitious

Working With Words

I. Fill in each blank with the appropriate word from the following list:

abominable	conjugal
pragmatic	ominous
adamantly	malapropism
sadist	disparaging
vegetate	venerated

She should have known. Jane's friends warned her that Count Villano was a (1)___*sadist*___ who derived pleasure from inflicting pain. Jane ignored stories of the count's (2)___*abomina*___, horrible cruelties. Villano charmed the plain-looking but wealthy Jane into tying the (3)___*conjugal*___ knot, but immediately following the marriage vows, the count whispered this (4)___*malapropism*___ to his bride, "I'll love you forever, my dreariest." This slip of the tongue—"dreariest" for "dearest"—was indeed (5)___*ominous*___ of the evil to come. Although not physically cruel to Jane, Count Villano would make (6)___*disparags*___ remarks about her appearance, mind, and personality. It became evident to Jane that the count's interest in her during courtship had not been romantic but (7)___*pragmatic*___—a mere practical desire to acquire her fortune. She now scorned the man she once (8)___*venerated*___ almost as a god. Count Villano left her to idle away her life and (9)___*vegetate*___ while he coldly ignored her, saving his passion for spending her wealth. Jane vowed revenge. (10)___*Adamantly*___ sticking to her plan, Jane refused to vegetate but cultivated a keen interest in vegetation—especially of the poisonous variety. Count Villano was eventually found dead, slumped over an exotic dish—you might say he received his just desserts.

II. Match the word on the left with its synonyms.

_____1. adamant   a. belittle, downgrade

_____2. pragmatic   b. foreboding, unfavorable

_____3. venerate   c. marital, married

_____4. malapropism   d. loathsome, horrible

_____5. sadistic   e. obdurate, unyielding

_____6. disparage   f. revere, honor

_____7. ominous   g. stagnate, be idle

_____8. vegetate   h. spoonerism, misusage

_____9. conjugal   i. utilitarian, practical

____10. abominable   j. perversely cruel, viscious

III. Word Part: SENT—feel, think (sentence, consent)

assent (uh SENT) *n.* agreement; *v.* agree

dissent (dih SENT) *n.* disagreement; *v.* disagree

presentiment (prih SEN tuh munt) *n.* vague expectation or feeling of
   something about to happen

sententious (sen TEN shus) *adj.* concise and full of meaning; using or
   full of proverbs and old sayings in a self- important, high-sounding,
   or boring way

sentiment (SEN tuh ment) *n.* feeling or opinion

Using each of the five SENT words only once, complete the following sentences.

1. Our neighbor may not have had a crystal ball, but every time she had a _____presentiment_____ that something bad would happen, it did.

2. Don't you have any feeling, opinion, or _____sentiment_____ about what I just said?

3. The dictator allowed no disagreement and would therefore tolerate no _____dissent_____.

4. If you _____assent_____ to my conditions, I will sign the contract.

5. The _____sententious_____ Polonious in Shakespeare's *Hamlet* continuously utters proverbs like "Neither a borrower, nor a lender be."

Chapter 6

1. despotic	6. trite
2. gullible	7. melancholy
3. guile	8. choleric
4. exonerate	9. phlegmatic
5. cliché	10. sanguine

1. *despotic* (des POT ik) *adj.* tyrannical, oppressive

In ancient Greece, *despotes* meant the family head, based on *domos* (house) + *posis* ("husband," "master"). The Greek *despotes* had powers far greater than the modern husband. These Greek household heads could even legally kill their wives and children, although such tyrannical exercise of authority rarely occurred. The Greeks also used *despotes* as a term for foreign rulers who had absolute control over their subjects. "Despot" then came to be the title of both emperors and high church officials in the Byzantine Empire. The modern negative and hostile sense of "despot" was reinforced by French revolutionaries, who applied the word to Louis XVI.

Alexander the Great and Kublai Kahn were famous despots. Football coaches and army sergeants sometimes exercise despotic control over their men. Twentieth-century American author Mary McCarthy stated, "Bureaucracy [rule by unquestioning, appointed officials], the rule of no one, has become the modern form of despotism." Patrick Henry declaimed against despotic British rule:

Is life so dear or peace so sweet as to be purchased at the price of chains and slavery? Forbid it, Almighty God! I know not what course others may take; but as for me, give me liberty, or give me death!

Synonyms: domineering, overbearing, dictatorial (dik tuh TOR ee ul)

Related words: autocratic, authoritarian, imperious, draconian

Contrasted words: egalitarian, lax

2. *gullible* (GUL uh bul) *adj.* easily deceived, tricked, cheated

A young, flightless bird—called a "gull" in some areas of England—can be easily tricked. The common water bird, the gull, will swallow almost anything. Perhaps these two types of gull helped form "gullible"; a gullible person swallows deceitful stories. Another possible source of "gullible" is the Latin word for throat (*gula*), suggesting the gulping down of whatever is offered. Although Jonathan Swift's *Gulliver's Travels* (1726) may not have been titled with "gull" in mind, gullible readers might have believed his tales of immense giants and minuscule people. Supposedly the circus owner P. T. Barnum commented on the gullibility of the general public: "There's a sucker born every minute." Swindlers and charlatans who gull or cheat their victims live by the motto: "Never give a sucker an even break."

Synonyms: trustful, naive, unsuspicious, credulous (KREJ uh lus)

Contrasted words: wary, sophisticated, shrewd, cynical, skeptical, astute

3. *guile* (GYL, rhymes with "smile") *n.* deceit, treachery

In a famous fairy tale, a beautiful but evil queen employs supernatural means to trick Snow White into eating a poisoned apple. Guile or trickery has long been associated with the supernatural, as in Frisian (a Germanic language) *wiglia*, a word meaning "sorcery" or "witchcraft" and related to our word "wile" ("cunning," "trickery") and its rhyming etymological cousin "guile." However, human beings need no otherworldly assistance to generate crafty deception as American poet Paul Laurence Dunbar (1872-1906) shows in "We Wear the Mask":

> We wear the mask that grins and lies,
> It hides our cheeks and shades our eyes,—
> This debt we pay to human guile;
> With torn and bleeding hearts we smile,
> And mouth with myriad [countless] subtleties.

The prejudices and unjust constraints of society unfortunately force us to mask our responses with deceitful cunning and guile.

Synonyms: slyness, cunning, trickery, deception, duplicity (doo PLIS uh tee)

Related words: chicanery, fraud, fraudulence, deviousness, wiliness, artifice

Contrasted words: candor, frankness, veracity, ingenuousness, naivete, artlessness

4. *exonerate* (ig ZON uh rate) *v.* free from blame

Whereas today's motorized vessels can haul huge amounts of cargo, ancient ships with their one or two sails struggled with much smaller loads. Sailors on these ancient ships felt relieved when they could unload and thus improve the performance of their crafts. The Latin word for this unloading was *exonerare*, from *ex* ("off") and *onus* ("burden"). When "exonerate" entered English, it assumed the general meaning of "relief from a burden," whether discharging goods from a ship or removing a load from one's shoulders. Lawyers then applied "exonerate" to their removing the burden of suspicion from the accused. So often did the courts use "exonerate" that today we employ the word solely in relation to freeing someone from the burden of guilt, blame, or responsibility of an action.

Pleading ignorance of the law will not exonerate one from a crime. During the famous Watergate scandal of the 1970's, the courts failed to exonerate President Richard Nixon's Attorney General John Mitchell and top aides John D. Ehrlichman and H. R. Haldeman from charges of perjury, obstruction of justice, and conspiracy; all three were sentenced to prison.

Synonyms: free, clear, pardon, justify, release, exculpate (EK skul pate)

Related words: vindicate, absolve, acquit

Contrasted words: incriminate, indict, censure

5. *cliché* (klee SHAY) *n.* expression or idea that is stale from overuse

Until about the middle of the nineteenth century, printers would drop a device into molten lead to produce type. The dropping would produce a clicking sound, and since French *clicher* means to "click," the French called the metal plate that contained the impression of the type a *cliché*. They also referred to the plate as a *stereotype* because it had a *stereo* (Greek for "solid," "three-dimensional") impression of the type. The *cliché* or *stereotype* would print the same thing over and over again and often be reused for some well-liked expression. Metaphorically, "cliché" came to mean any overworked expression that has lost its vigor. Similarly, "stereotype" assumed the general meaning of an oversimplified, fixed, standardized conception that allows for no individual differences. Prejudice feeds on racial, religious, and national stereotypes. Conscientious writers avoid clichés such as "slept like a log," "bored to death," "pretty as a picture," "every cloud has a silver lining," and "whatever will be will be."

Synonyms: overused expression, overworked expression, platitude (PLAT uh tood)

Related words: triteness, banality, bromide, stereotype

6. *trite* (TRITE) *adj.* uninteresting because of overuse; lacking originality and freshness

A new car, new shoes, even a newly minted penny attract us with their sparkling freshness. How different the appearance of a battered automobile, old shoes, and a much handled coin. From Latin *tritus* ("rubbed away," "worn out"), we get "trite" that aptly describes worn-out phrases, overused plots, and dull, commonplace ideas. "Hackneyed"—a synonym of "trite"—comes from Hackney, a town near London once famous for its horses and carriages, both of which came to be called "hackneys." Because the horses often did laborious, repetitive work, "hackney" acquired the meaning "overwork." Finally, "hackneyed" assumed its present sense of worn-out, stale, overworked. Clichés are trite and hackneyed expressions.

Synonyms: well-worn, stale, commonplace, hackneyed (HAK need)

Related words: clichéd, banal, pedestrian, stereotyped, stereotypical, platitudinous, bromidic, bathetic

Contrasted words: novel, seminal, unique

7. *melancholy* (MEL un kol ee) *adj.* sad, gloomy, depressed; *n.* sadness, gloom, depression

8. *choleric* (KOL uh rik, kuh LER ik) *adj.* easily angered; grouchy; quick-tempered

9. *phlegmatic* (fleg MAT ik) *adj.* sluggish, not easily excited

10. *sanguine* (SANG gwin) *adj.* cheerful, confident, hopeful

Our ancestors strove for harmony with the universe. Traditional Oriental philosophy, psychology, and medicine stressed a proper balance between the passive or female principle called "yin" and the active or male principle called "yang." Similarly, for about two thousand years, the Western world from the ancient Greeks to the Renaissance thought that health and personality were determined by the relation of four vital liquids called "humors" (Latin *humor* meant "fluid," "moisture"). These humors were blood, phlegm, choler (yellow bile), and melancholy (black bile; *melan* is the Greek combining form for "black"). Excess blood (Latin *sanguis* = "blood") produced a cheerful or sanguine disposition; too much phlegm made one unemotional or phlegmatic; an abundance of bile disposed an individual to be angry, quick-tempered, or choleric; a surplus of black bile resulted in a brooding, depressing, melancholy personality. Whereas a proper balance of the four humors produced a healthy personality, too much of any one humor made one "humorous" or odd, hence somewhat comical or laughable, resulting eventually in the modern meaning of "humor."

We picture Santa Claus as cheerful or sanguine, and Grumpy in "Snow White and the Seven Dwarfs" as choleric. However, the savage appearance of the English bulldog belies his sluggish, unexcitable, phlegmatic nature. Perhaps the most famous example of a gloomy, thoughtful, melancholy personality is Shakespeare's Hamlet, whom Renaissance audiences recognized as having an excess of melancholy humor. Another of Shakespeare's "humorous" characters—the melancholy Jacques in *As You Like It*—delivers these famous melancholy lines:

> All the world's a stage,
> And all the men and women merely players;
> They have their exits and their entrances,
> And one man in his time plays many parts,
> His acts being seven ages. At first, the infant
> Mewling and puking in the nurse's arms.
> Then the whining schoolboy, with his satchel
> And shining morning face, creeping like snail
> Unwillingly to school. And then the lover,
> Sighing like furnace, with a woeful ballad
> Made to his mistress' eyebrow. Then a soldier,
> Full of strange oaths and bearded like the pard [leopard],
> Jealous in honor, sudden and quick in quarrel,
> Seeking the bubble reputation
> Even in the cannon's mouth. And then the justice,
> In fair round belly with good capon lined,
> With eyes severe and beard of formal cut,
> Full of wise saws [sayings] and modern instances;
> And so he plays his part. The sixth age shifts
> Into the lean and slippered pantaloon [ridiculous old man],
> With spectacles on nose and pouch on side;

His youthful hose, well saved, a world too wide
For his shrunk shank, and his big manly voice,
Turning again toward childish treble, pipes
And whistles in his sound. Last scene of all,
That ends this strange eventful history,
Is second childishness and mere oblivion,
Sans [without] teeth, sans eyes, sans everything.

Synonyms for "melancholy" (*adj.*): saddened, unhappy, mournful, plaintive (PLAYN tiv)

Related words for "melancholy" (*adj.*): doleful, dejected, despondent, somber, dismal, glum, disconsolate

Contrasted words for "melancholy" (*adj.*): exhilarated, exhilarating, vivacious, euphoric

Synonyms for "choleric": cranky, hot-tempered, irascible (ih RAS uh bul)

Related words for "choleric": irate, testy, petulant, splenetic, peevish

Contrasted words for "choleric": serene, tranquil, placid

Synonyms for "phlegmatic": dull, unemotional, unexcitable, stolid (STOL id)

Related words for "phlegmatic": imperturbable, apathetic, indifferent, undemonstrative, impassive, lethargic, listless, languid, placid

Contrasted words for "phlegmatic": animated, demonstrative, sanguine

Synonyms for "sanguine": positive, assured, optimistic (op tuh MIS tik)

Related word for "sanguine": buoyant

Contrasted words for "sanguine": melancholy, pessimistic, cynical, somber, despondent, morose, saturnine

Working With Words

I. Fill in each blank with the appropriate word from the following list:

sanguine	exonerate
guile	phlegmatic
clichés	choleric
gullible	trite
despotic	melancholy

Each word must be used only once.

His beloved father dead, his mother soon remarrying an uncle he despises—no wonder Shakespeare's Hamlet, Prince of Denmark, is gloomy, sad, depressed—in a word, (1)___melancholy___. To make matters worse, a ghost claiming to be Hamlet's father declares the uncle a murderer. Not (2)___gullible___ or easily deceived, Hamlet must prove to himself whether his uncle really killed his father. The prince devises a trap in the form of a play portraying a murder like that described by the ghost. If the uncle—now his stepfather and king— reacts strangely when seeing the play, Hamlet will know that his uncle is the murderer. The father of Hamlet's girlfriend, the high court official Polonius, hopes that the prince will be more cheerful and (3)___sanguine___ while directing the actors of this play. Polonius himself is a comical figure who constantly gives stale, commonplace, (4)___trite___ advice in the form of overworked expressions or (5)___clichés___. Hamlet sometimes mocks the babbling Polonius, but Polonius never becomes angry, quick-tempered, or (6)___choleric___. Finally, Hamlet presents the play to the court. The uncle violently reacts to the murder scene, thus revealing his treacherous deceit and (7)___guile___; Hamlet now knows his uncle to be a murderer. Because the play failed to (8)___exonerate___ his uncle, Hamlet determines revenge. Wary of Hamlet, the uncle nevertheless cannot take bold, aggressive action against his nephew because this would make the king seem tyrannical and (9)___despotic___, perhaps inciting angry reaction from the masses who love the prince. Instead, the uncle guilefully manages to send Hamlet on a journey whose planned end is assassination. Hamlet discovers the plot, escapes, and returns home. However, Hamlct still lingeringly contemplates revenge but never takes decisive action. Some may begin to despair that Hamlet's sluggish, dull, (10)_____ response to his father's murder will never lead to satisfying revenge. But when pricked by the point of a poisonous fencing blade, Hamlet at last reaches his own decisive point, concentrates his remaining energy, and slays the king.

II. Match the word on the left with its synonyms.

_____1. guile   a. stolid, sluggish

_____2. phlegmatic   b. irascible, grouchy

_____3. melancholy   c. dictatorial, tyrannical

_____4. sanguine   d. credulous, naive

_____5. cliché   e. optimistic, cheerful

_____6. gullible   f. plaintive, sad

_____7. choleric   g. duplicity, deceit

_____8. trite   h. exculpate, free

_____9. despotic   i. hackneyed, stale

___10. exonerate   j. platitude, overused expression

III. Word Part: SENS—feel, think (sense, sensation, sensitive)

consensus (kun SEN sus) *n.* general agreement, majority opinion, harmony

dissension (dih SEN shun) *n.* strong disagreement, quarreling

sensual (SEN shoo ul) *adj.* enjoying bodily pleasures; pertaining to the body and the senses rather than the mind or spirit *insensible* (in SEN suh bul) *adj.* unable to feel; unaware; unconscious

insensitivity (in sen suh TIV uh tee) *n.* inability to be affected by; lack of sensitivity

Using each of the five SENS words only once, complete the following sentences.

1. There was much disagreement, protest, and _____ about the Vietnam War.

2. The minister criticized the rich, greedy members of the community for their _____ to the hardships of the poor.

3. After long hours of debate, the committee finally reached a common agreement or _____ on what should be done.

4. Whereas my oldest brother likes nothing better than solving abstract mathematical problems and pondering philosophical questions, my _____ younger brother delights in eating, drinking, and dating.

5. When my uncle was told he had won the grand prize in the city lottery for ten million dollars, he fainted—_____ to the congratulations of relatives and friends.

Chapter 7

1. maverick   6. hedonist

2. esoteric   7. nihilist

3. undermine   8. somnolent

4. alleviate   9. diatribe

5. bacchanal   10. tribulation

1. *maverick* (MAV uh rik) *n.* independent person

In 1845 Texas lawyer Samuel Augustus Maverick received four hundred head of cattle to settle a client's $1200 debt. Uninterested in the cattle business, Maverick failed to brand his animals and let them stray. Other ranchers were quick to put their brand on Maverick's strays. Eventually, Maverick sold his dwindling herd. Although he suffered a financial loss on his cattle, Maverick enriched our language. Unbranded calves and other unbranded range animals came to be called mavericks and, by extension, independent persons taking positions different than their associates also came to be labeled mavericks.

Political mavericks refuse to conform to a party line; artistic mavericks shatter accepted conventions and stereotypes; scientific mavericks forge revolutionary theories. Always a maverick, the all-American football player and internationally acclaimed singer and actor (who starred in Shakespeare's *Othello* and Eugene O'Neill's *The Emperor Jones*) Paul Robeson (1898-1976) continually jeopardized his career to support movements for world peace, improved labor conditions, and racial justice.

Synonyms: individualist, independent thinker, nonconformist (non kun
FOR mist)

Related words: dissenter, dissident, apostate, bohemian, eccentric

2. *esoteric* (es uh TER ik) *adj.* known or understood only by a select
few

In geometry we learn the Pythagorean theorum, which states that in a
right triangle the square of the hypotenuse equals the sum of the squares
of the other two sides. We represent this theorum by the formula $a^2 +$
$b^2 = c^2$ where c is the hypotenuse and a and b the two sides. Pythagoras,
the ancient Greek mathematician after whom this theorum was named,
was also a teacher of philosophical and religious principles. He believed
that after death our souls seek out another body in which we are reborn,
a doctrine known as reincarnation or the transmigration of the soul and
still part of the faith of many Hindus in India. Pythagoras taught most
of his students from behind a curtain so that they could only hear his
voice; but a select few—his innermost (*esoterikos* in Greek) students—
were allowed behind the curtain. To this inner circle of disciples within
the veil, Pythagoras revealed his secret doctrines. Hence, today
"esoteric" refers to obscure or difficult systems of thought, perplexing
literary or artistic works, or any knowledge understood by only a few.
Whereas many are familiar with the Pythagorean theorum, few know
the esoteric association of Pythagoras with the etymology of "esoteric."
Ironically, "esoteric" is not an esoteric word among educated people,
but its antonym "exoteric"—meaning "popular," "understood by the
many"—is rarely used and can be considered an esoteric word.

Synonyms: secret, mysterious, difficult, deep, profound, obscure,
abstruse (ab STROOS)

Related words: recondite, arcane, cabalistic, cryptic, inscrutable, enig-
matic, occult

Contrasted words: intelligible, accessible, exoteric

3. *undermine* (un der MINE) *v.* weaken gradually; injure or destroy
   secretly or underhandedly; dig beneath or wear away from under

"Undermine" entered our language in the fourteenth century to
describe the process by which attacking soldiers dug a mine or tunnel
under the walls of a castle. These tunnels either helped topple the walls
or enabled the soldiers to burrow their way into the fortress. Today, we
still speak of a flood undermining the foundation of a house. However,
opponents can metaphorically undermine one's plans by creating
obstacles. Poor diet, lack of fresh air, and stress undermine health. As
Scotland's national poet Robert Burns (1759-1796) says in "To a
Mouse," unforeseen incidents undermine the most carefully designed
programs:

> The best laid schemes o' mice an' men
> Gang aft a-gley [go often wrong].

Synonyms: weaken, disable, cripple, undercut, sabotage (SAB uh tahj
   [rhymes with "garage"])

Related words: erode, subvert, foil, thwart, enfeeble, debilitate, vitiate,
   impair

Contrasted words: sustain, fortify, buttress

4. *alleviate* (uh LEE vee ate) *v.* relieve; lessen or make more bearable
   (pain, evil, suffering)

Whereas in modern hospitals a doctor or nurse raises the newborn child
to its mother's arms, ancient Romans endowed this act with divinity by
having Levana—goddess of childbirth—gently lift the infant to its awaiting mother. Levana's name describes her function since Latin *levare*
means "lighten, lift, raise." Of course, modern technology alleviates or
relieves many of our burdens, as when a department store elevator
("elevator" also derives from *levare*) easily lifts a mother with her
scrambling children and many packages. Friendly bankers alleviate
financial problems, physicians alleviate bodily aches and pains, and
psychiatrists alleviate mental torment.

Synonyms: ease, lighten, reduce, mitigate (MIT uh gate)

Related words: assuage, palliate, mollify, allay

Contrasted words: augment, aggravate, enhance, exacerbate

5. *bacchanal* (bak uh NAL), *bacchanalia* (bak uh NAIL yuh) *n.* wild, drunken party

> Drink to me only with thine eyes,
>   And I will pledge with mine;
> Or leave a kiss but in the cup
>   And I'll not look for wine.
> (from "To Celia" by Ben Jonson)

Humans, however, have sought intoxicating beverages since time immemorial. The ancient Greeks and Romans worshipped the god of wine; the Greeks called him Dionysus, the Romans Bacchus. In one myth, Dionysus comes to Thebes only to be scorned and imprisoned by the king. Easily escaping, Dionysus takes savage revenge by making the king's mother and sisters mad so that they believe him to be a wild lion. When the king encounters them in the forest, they attack him and tear apart his limbs. Too late they recover from their madness to discover their loved one's mutilated body. Dionysus or Bacchus was associated with madness and frenzy, but also with inspiration (reflecting the dual nature of wine), for the soul-stirring Greek tragedies were outgrowths of sacred festivities honoring Dionysus. In Rome, however, festivals of Bacchus eventually degenerated into drunken, sexually unrestrained, riotous behavior known as *bacchanalia*, hence giving us the words "bacchanal" and "bacchanalia." So wild were these bacchanalian ceremonies that the Roman senate banned them in 186 B.C.

Synonyms: party, feast, merrymaking, overindulgence, spree, orgy (OR jee)

Related words: revelry, carousal, saturnalia, debauch

6. *hedonist* (HEE doh nist) *n.* one who lives only for pleasure

We love our sweethearts, delight in sweet dreams, and savor the sweet smell of success. Even the Greek gods had a sweet tooth, for their drink was nectar. No wonder that the origin of hedonism, the belief that pleasure is the chief good of life, is related to the Greek word for sweet—*hedys*. Somewhat similar in meaning to "hedonist" is "epicure" ("gourmet or one who delights in and has discriminating taste regarding good food and drink"). Whereas "epicurean" describes a lover of luxurious, sensual pleasures, the Greek philosopher Epicurus (341-270 B.C.)—from whom the word is derived—lived quite modestly. True, he advocated pleasure as the chief goal of life, but identified pleasure with peace of mind and a healthy body free from pain. He actually taught that we must forgo immediate sensual gratification to attain long term pleasures of mental tranquility and physical health. To this end, his usual diet was mainly water and barley bread. However, his doctrine of pleasure came to be associated with fasting and the luxurious life, so that the fourteenth-century English poet Chaucer thus describes the Franklin (a wealthy landowner) in *The Canterbury Tales*:

> Well loved he in the morning bread soaked in wine.
> To live in sensual pleasure was ever his custom,
> For he was Epicurus' own son
> That held opinion that total pleasure
> Was true, perfect bliss.

Another word for one devoted to pleasure is "sybarite." The Sybarites were ancient Greek colonists famous for their wealthy, sensual living— jet-setters of their day practicing Hugh Hefner's playboy philosophy. One Sybarite complained that he could not sleep because he was bothered by a rose petal doubled beneath him. Presumably, the Sybarites—who had taught their horses to dance to musical pipes— were conquered by an invading army which piped tunes that threw the native horses into prancing disorder. Whereas "hedonist" and "sybarites" are strong terms reserved for those who wallow in pleasure, "epicure" is the most suitable term for one with refined taste in wining and dining. Hedonistic, sybaritic, and epicurean individuals all follow the motto: "Eat, drink, and be merry."

Synonyms: pleasure seeker, playboy, playgirl, jet-setter, sybarite (SIB uh rite)

Related words: epicure, voluptuary, sensualist, libertine, dissipater, profligate, debauchee

Contrasted words: ascetic, Spartan, puritan, moralist

7. *nihilist* (NY [rhymes with "cry"] uh list, NEE uh list) *n.* one who rejects all religious, moral, and traditional values, practices, and institutions

Agnostics do not know whether or not God exists, atheists definitely do not believe in God, and nihilists do not believe in anything at all. Nihilism is the total denial of values, laws, and restraints. Nihilists reject all religious and moral principles, all political and social institutions. Appropriately enough, "nihilist" derives from *nihil*, the Latin word for "nothing."

Ivan Turgenev—like Tolstoy and Dostoevsky a great nineteenth-century Russian novelist—popularized "nihilism" in *Fathers and Sons*. A young medical student—the nihilist of the novel—spurns all traditional beliefs, sneering at sentiments such as "love." However, he falls passionately and incurably for a woman who rejects him. Ultimately, the nihilist dies from exposure to typhus infection, perhaps with the implication that a broken heart might have made him careless when examining the contagious disease. Just as nihilism undermines society, so may a rejection of all values undermine the psychological soundness of the individual nihilist. Akin to nihilism is anarchy (absence of government or law; chaos, confusion disorder). Anarchists strive to overthrow government and all official regulation. The poet W. B. Yeats forecast the nihilistic collapse of civilization in "The Second Coming":

> Things fall apart; the center cannot hold;
> Mere anarchy is loosed upon the world.

Synonyms: doubter, disbeliever, pessimist, revolutionary, rebel, anarchist (AN ur kist)

Related words: skeptic, iconoclast, radical

8. *somnolent* (SOM nuh lunt) *adj.* sleepy, drowsy; causing sleep

Sleep and dreams have always fascinated humans. The biblical Joseph accurately interpreted the Pharaoh's dream of seven lean cows swallowing seven fat cows as seven years of prosperity followed by seven years of famine. Ancient Greek oracles at Delphi had special marble dreaming-beds to help guide their prophecies. The Greeks and Romans personified the realm of sleeping visions in Morpheus, god of dreams (hence, the painkilling drug morphine). The Greek god of sleep Hypnos gives us the word "hypnotism." Romans called the god of sleep Somnus. When we can't sleep, we have insomnia (from Latin *in* = "not," *somnus* = "sleep"). Somnambulism is sleepwalking. Sominex is an appropriately named sleeping pill, inducing somnolence or sleep. A somnolent sermon causes drowsiness or sleep. Somnolent or sleepy children drowsily rub their eyes listening to soothing bedtime stories. Perhaps you have had enough explanation, and this account is making you somnolent. If not, savor these lines from the great Irish poet W. B. Yeats' "Sailing to Byzantium" in which the narrator tells how after his soul sheds its decaying body in death, it will seek some immortal, artistic form such as kept somnolent Byzantine emperors awake:

> Once out of nature I shall never take
> My bodily form from any natural thing,
> But such a form as Grecian goldsmiths make
> Of hammered gold or gold enameling
> To keep a drowsy Emperor awake.

Synonyms: sleepy, drowsy, lulling, slumberous, soporific (sop uh RIF ik)

Related words: torpid, lethargic, sedated, sedative

Contrasted words: invigorating, animated

9. *diatribe* (DY uh tribe) *n.* violent, angry, bitter attack in words

10. *tribulation* (trib yuh LAY shun) *n.*   great suffering, misery, or
    distress

Ancient Romans dragged a heavy studded board called *tribulum* over
wheat in order to separate grain from husk. An early Christian writer
saw a metaphorical relationship between this process (*tribulatio* in
Latin) and the grief, suffering, and hardships that press down on
believers to refine and purify their grain of faith. Hence, "tribulation"
refers to trials, burdens, and miseries that wear us down. "Diatribe,"
from Greek *dia* ("away," "through") + *tribein* ("wear," "rub,"), also
conveys the concept of something worn away—in this case time worn
away by a barrage of talk. Of course, employers of diatribe or abusive
criticism aim not to waste time but to "waste" or "rub out" their victims.
Reformers for women's rights and racial equality like Susan B. Anthony
and Frederick Douglass often had to bear the tribulations of vicious
diatribe.

Synonyms for "diatribe": verbal abuse, denunciation, tirade (TY rade)

Related words for "diatribe": invective, harangue, jeremiad, philippic,
    vituperation, castigation, contumely

Contrasted words for "diatribe": encomium, panegyric, paean

Synonyms for "tribulation": ordeal, trouble, sorrow, hardship, affliction
    (uh FLIK shun)

Related words for "tribulation": adversity, travail

Contrasted words for "tribulation": jubilation, ecstasy, consolation,
    solace

Working With Words

I. Fill in each blank with the appropriate word from the following list:

hedonistic   diatribes

somnolent   esoteric

bacchanals   undermining

alleviated   nihilist

maverick   tribulations

Each word must be used only once.

All his life John Strait had worked hard. When his father died, John (1)_____ *alleviated* his mother's financial burden by leaving college for a job to support his three younger brothers. During the following years, John endured much hardship and suffered many (2)_____ *tribulations* , but intense effort and willpower paid off. He eventually became the owner of a successful restaurant chain. John determined that his children would have everything he could afford. The children, however, had plans of their own. His eldest daughter—an extremely independent person, a true (3) *maverick* —refused the offer of a luxurious summer vacation in a palace on the Mediterranean and instead left with her boyfriend to do volunteer social work in a poor farm area in Central America. His youngest daughter would often disappear for several weeks to study some secret, (4)_____ *esoteric* teachings of a foreign sorcerer or magician. His boys caused even more tribulation. The eldest son became a violent opponent of any form of government, a (5) *nihilist* who believed in no spiritual, social, or political restraints. Sadly, John would continually have to bail this child out of jail. The middle son shocked John's conservative sense of decency by partaking in wild, drunken (6)_____ *bacchanals* . A stern, sacrificing father, John could never understand this pleasure-seeking, (7)_____ *hedonistic* son. The poor man thought that his children were (8)_____ *undermining* everything he had worked for. His bitter, angry lectures or (9)_____ *diatribes* to his children had no effect. But his heart attack did. The only child home at the time—the youngest son, usually a lazy, drowsy, (10)_____ *somnolent* boy who slept during most of the day as well as at night—amazingly rushed to the hospital and stayed caringly alert for several days at his father's side. The other children soon came to alleviate this family tribulation. John's crisis brought out their desire to work where needed, something John's sheltering security had always denied them. As John fortunately recovered, he realized that it is no esoteric mystery but a simple truth that everyone needs to feel needed.

II. Match the word on the left with its synonyms.

___ 1. esoteric	a. tirade, verbal abuse
___ 2. tribulation	b. anarchist, disbeliever
___ 3. bacchanal	c. soporific, sleepy
___ 4. undermine	d. nonconformist, individualist
___ 5. maverick	e. affliction, suffering
___ 6. hedonist	f. mitigate, relieve
___ 7. somnolent	g. sabotage, undercut
___ 8. diatribe	h. abstruse, mysterious
___ 9. nihilist	i. sybarite, pleasure seeker
___ 10. alleviate	j. orgy, wild party

III. Word Part: VERT—turn (convert, pervert)

avert (uh VURT) *v.* turn away; prevent

divert (dih VURT, dy VURT) *v.* turn aside from a purpose, course, path; distract; amuse

subvert (sub VURT) *v.* overthrow (something established); undermine

revert (rih VURT) *v.* return to a former condition

vertigo (VUR tuh goh) *n.* dizziness

Using each of the five VERT words only once, complete the following sentences.

1. Isaac Newton possessed enormous powers of concentration; nothing could _____ his attention while he was solving a scientific problem.

2. The mayor complained that his political opponents were trying to defeat or _____ his efforts to reform the community.

3. After severe dieting, many of us _____ to our old eating habits.

4. A good way to _____ an accident is to drive defensively.

5. I avoid the dizzy, spinning rides at amusement parks in order to avert _____.

Chapter 8

1. paradox
2. admonish
3. penitent
4. accolade
5. nonchalant

6. banal
7. iridescent
8. cajole
9. urbane
10. stymie

1. *paradox* (PAR uh dox) *n.* seemingly self-contradictory statement (possibly true), condition, or person

Children sometimes playfully ask, "If God can do anything, can He make a stone so heavy that He cannot lift it?" The question poses a paradoxical situation. If God can do anything, then He can create an unliftable stone, but if He cannot lift the stone, then He cannot do everything. On a more serious level, the Christian concept of the Trinity is a paradox, for God is both one and three. A famous ancient Greek paradox is Zeno's paradox. It shows that in a race if a tortoise has a lead, a man can never catch it. When the man reaches the point from which the tortoise started, the tortoise has already moved on to a second point. When the man reaches this second point, the tortoise has already moved to a third point, and so on forever. With this logic one can paradoxically show that the man will never catch the tortoise although in reality runners (or even walkers) can easily overtake tortoises. Paradoxically, we can hate those we love. Portrayer of the Roaring Twenties in such works as his novel *The Great Gatsby*, F. Scott Fitzgerald was a paradox who hungered for wealth while simultaneously keenly aware of the superficiality of material success. As we can see, "paradox" is true to its Greek elements *para* ("beside," "beyond," "contrary to,") and *doxa* ("opinion") which formed Greek *paradoxos* ("beyond belief," "unbelievable"). A special form of paradox is a Catch-22, a contradiction in which one is caught between conflicting orders or regulations. "Catch-22" derives from Joseph Heller's novel *Catch-22*. The novel describes how overworked American World War II pilots flying dangerous missions could be relieved of duty if they were judged insane. A pilot, however, could not be relieved of duty if he asked not to fly for fear of getting killed, because rules stated that anyone refusing to fly to avoid death must be sane. Thus, a pilot "would be crazy to fly more missions and sane if he didn't, but if he was sane he had to fly them. If he flew them he was crazy and didn't have to; but if he didn't want to he was sane and had to." A common Catch-22 is when someone without experience seeks a job and is told that only experienced workers are hired. How then can anyone get experience in order to be hired?

Synonyms: contradiction, inconsistency, Catch-22

2. *admonish* (ad MON ish) *v.* warn, advise, or criticize to correct a fault

"Admonish" clearly goes back to its Latin elements *ad* ("to") + *monere* ("advise," "warn"). We are all familiar with class and hall monitors who warn, advise, and look over us. The prophet Nathan delivered one of the most famous biblical admonitions or critical warnings to King David. Falling in love with Bathsheba, David ordered his commanding officer to send Bathsheba's husband to the battle front and then withdraw supporting troops. After the husband was slain, Nathan came to David and told him a story about a rich man possessing numerous flocks and herds and a poor man owning but one little female lamb. In order to feed a traveler, the rich man—unwilling to reduce his own herds or flocks—took the poor man's little lamb and served it to the guest. Enraged at this greedy act, David declared that the rich man deserved to die. Nathan then said admonishingly to David, "You are the man." Instantly, guilt and remorse overwhelmed David. Nathan's admonishing story struck home. As God's spokesman, Nathan loved David but hated the sin. His stern admonishment or rebuke and scolding was meant to correct the wayward king.

Synonyms: scold, caution, counsel, urge, rebuke, reprove (rih PROOV)

Related words: reprimand, reproach, exhort, chide, censure, berate, upbraid

Contrasted words: commend, acclaim, extol

3. *penitent* (PEN uh tunt) *adj.* feeling sorry and willing to atone or make up for sin or wrongdoing

In times past churches provided a special room called a "penitentiary" for those wanting to atone or make up for some sin. A priest would direct repentant or regretful sinners to atone for their sins by fasting for several days or performing long hours of prayer in the penitentiary. The repentant sinners were known as "penitents" from "penitentiary." Hence, the adjectives "penitent" and "penitential" assumed the meaning of "sorry for offenses."

Not until about 1800 was "penitentiary" used synonymously with "prison." Before this time, people were rarely imprisoned as punishment for their crimes. Instead, they stayed in prison while waiting for their trial or sentence. Common punishments for criminals were fines, whipping, branding, forced labor as an oarsman on a ship called a "galley," and execution. Prison reforms during the late eighteenth-century transformed prisons into places of confinement where convicted inmates would feel sorry or penitent for their crimes. "Penitentiary" thus came to have its modern meaning.

Insane with jealousy, King Leontes in Shakespeare's *The Winter's Tale* accuses his devoted wife of adultery with his best friend, prepares her for a humiliating public trial, then learns of her death. Recovering his sanity, Leontes penitently mourns for the next sixteen years so that his ministers refer to him as "the penitent king." In a fairy tale ending, the king approaches what he thinks is a realistic sculpture of his queen, only to discover that it is really his wife who has been safely hidden from him these many years. Purified through penance, King Leontes reunites with his beloved.

Synonyms: sorry, repentant, conscience-stricken, contrite (kun TRITE)

Related words: remorseful, atoning

Contrasted words: impenitent, unrepentant, unregenerate, remorseless

4. *accolade* (AK uh lade) *n.* high praise, award, honor

"Accolade" entered the English language meaning the ceremonial granting of knighthood with an embrace, kiss, and tap on the shoulder with the flat of a sword. Originally, "accolade" derives form Latin *ac* (variant of *ad*, "to") and *collum* ("neck"), an embrace being a throwing of the arms around someone's neck. Today, "accolade" is used in the general sense of great praise, honored recognition, enthusiastic approval. Applause, medals, and praise are forms of accolade.

At the beginning of their writing careers, William Golding and William Faulkner encountered many discouraging rejections of their works, but both went on to receive numerous accolades, including the Nobel prize. A synonym for "accolade" is "laurels," stemming from an ancient Greek myth about Apollo—god of light, medicine, and poetry—and Daphne, his first love. Apollo spied the maiden in a forest and instantly pursued her. Frightened, Daphne fled but the passionate Apollo dashed after her. As the god narrowed the gap, Daphne prayed to her father—a river god—to save her. To prevent Apollo from taking his daughter, the river god transformed her into a laurel tree. Broken-hearted, Apollo declared that the laurel would henceforth be his special tree, its leaves honoring the brows of the victors at his festivals. The laurel became the symbol of triumph for Greeks and Romans. "Laureate" is "one crowned with honor," as a Nobel laureate or poet laureate.

Although the famous old painter was showered with a plethora or superabundance of accolades and laurels, he felt most rewarded when his little grandson hugged him around the neck and said, "I like your paintings, Grandpa!"—a most etymologically appropriate form of accolade.

Synonyms: acclaim, tribute, recognition, praise, laurels (LAWR ulz)

Related words: commendation, kudos

Contrasted word: censure

5. *nonchalant* (non shuh LAHNT) *adj.*   casually unconcerned

Bullets, bombs, "broads"—nothing ruffles or disturbs the fictitious British secret service agent James Bond. Since he confronts danger with nonchalance—from Latin *non* ("not") + *calore* ("be warm")—he always maintains his "cool." Students who nonchalantly fail to prepare for classes may encounter a heated response from teachers and parents. Interestingly, the first recorded use of the adjective "nonchalant" is by the English Romantic poet Lord Byron in 1813. Few of his contemporaries, however, could be nonchalant about Byron, notorious for his scandalous love affairs and described by one lover as "mad, bad, and dangerous to know."

Synonyms: unconcerned, cool, casual, easygoing, carefree, indifferent, insouciant (in SOO see unt)

Related words: imperturbable, unruffled, debonair

Contrasted words: perturbed, disconcerted, apprehensive, fretful, agitated

6. *banal* (buh NAL, BAY nul) *adj.*   ordinary, uninteresting, pointless

A feudal lord in the Middle Ages compelled his tenants to use his facilities—ovens, winepress, farm tools, animal pens, storage shelters, mills, etc.—on the lord's terms. The French word referring to the right of the lord to decree this compulsory service was *banal*. From something forced, "banal" came to mean "commonplace" since everyone used the *banal* facilities. People tire of hearing the same old banalities spouted by unimaginative political candidates. The real horror of evil is not its shocking ghastliness but its banality as we become habituated to exploitation and injustice. A stale, lifeless, banal comment could also be described as "insipid"—from Latin *in* = "not" + *sapidus* = "tasty"— hence dull or tasteless. Although grammatically perfect, a student's essay may receive a mediocre grade because of the insipid style and banal thought.

Synonyms: commonplace, unoriginal, unimaginative, insipid (in SIP id)

Related words: trite, hackneyed, pedestrian, prosaic, vapid, stereotyped, platitudinous, jejune

Contrasted words: innovative, provocative, novel, unique

7. *iridescent* (ir uh DES unt) *adj.* showing rainbow-like colors

The ancients felt the sacredness of the beautiful, heavenly rainbow. God's sign to Noah that there would never again be a flood to destroy the earth was the rainbow. By placing His weapon or rainbow in the sky—the bow from which God shot the lightnings of his arrows—God showed that his anger had ended. For the ancient Greeks, Iris was the rainbow goddess and, along with Hermes (called Mercury by the Romans), was the messenger of the gods. Iris gave her name to the iris or colorful part of the eye and to the large, beautifully colored iris flower. Also from Iris derives "iridescent," meaning "glittering, glistening, brilliant with color." "Iridescent" refers to a shining display of many colors, such as an iridescent soap bubble sparkling in the sun or an iridescent costume glittering on stage. By looking through a prism, we can observe the iridescence of sunlight. "Iridescent" may also apply to a dazzling performance. In iridescent prose, James Baldwin warned the United States in *The Fire Next Time* to end racial strife in order to avoid the fulfillment of this prophecy from a slave song:

> God gave Noah the rainbow sign,
> No more water, the fire next time.

Synonyms: glistening, glittering, colorful, brilliant, lustrous (LUS trus)

Related words: opalescent, prismatic, polychromatic, radiant, luminous, effulgent

Contrasted words: lackluster, drab

8. *cajole* (kuh JOL) *v.* persuade by flattery, promises, pleasant or misleading words

Medieval Frenchman often caged the European jay, a cousin of the American blue jay, for a household pet. The jay would beg, plead, and whine with its harsh shrill until fed to its satisfaction—hence French *cajoler* ("chatter like a caged jay"). Today, one who similarly gets a person to do something by begging, pleading, promising, or "sweet-talking" employs cajolery. The old expression "you can catch more flies with honey than with vinegar" implies that sweet, cajoling speech can often get more accomplished than harsh threats. Beware of sales persons who attempt to cajole you into buying their products. If you have not read Maya Angelou's *I Know Why the Caged Bird Sings*, you might think I am mentioning it to cajole you into reading about the etymological connection between "cajolery" and the shrill singing caged jaybird. Wrong. No cajolery should be necessary, however, to entice you to read this powerfully evocative autobiographical account of how a sensitive, gifted Black girl growing up in Arkansas during the 1930's and 40's triumphed over adversities such as rape and racial humiliation.

Synonyms: persuade, flatter, coax (COKES)

Related words: wheedle, blandish, entice, inveigle, beguile

Contrasted words: extort, coerce

9. **urbane** (ur BANE) *adj.* sophisticated, smooth, polite, polished in manner

City dwellers have historically looked down upon country folk. This snobbery can be seen in the words "urbane" and "villain." "Urbane," as does "urban" and "suburban," comes from Latin *urbs* ("city"). "Urban" still retains the literal root meaning of "city," but "urbane" has been elevated to mean "refined," "cultivated," "knowledgeably gracious." Evidently, city folks thought highly of themselves. They thought little of the farm laborer (Latin *villanus*), so little that *villanus* gave rise to our word "villain." Of course, we are all familiar through films with slick, suave, sophisticated villains, although an urbane villain is somewhat of an etymological contradiction.

The gentleman's urbane wit was wasted on his crude, uneducated audience. Sophisticated taste in clothes, food, and entertainment characterizes urbanity. Common folk who value substance over style may prefer the plain to the urbane.

Synonyms: refined, cultivated, smooth, courteous, elegant, suave (SWAHV)

Related words: cosmopolitan, debonair

Contrasted words: gauche, uncouth, boorish

10. *stymie* (STY mee) *v.* block, hinder, frustrate

Health experts tell us that to relieve ourselves from the pressures of work we should seek recreation. Those who seek relief on the golf course from some perplexing, confusing, or frustrating business problem may, however, find themselves literally stymied. "Stymie" is a golfing term for when an opponent's ball lies on a direct line between the putter's ball and the hole. From a specific golfing term for the blocking of a putter's ball, "stymie" acquired the general meaning of "block," "hinder," "confuse."

Have you ever been stymied or baffled by some problem in mathematics? Sherlock Holmes solved many crimes that stymied Scotland Yard. The new principal was stymied by striking teachers, a hostile press, and inadequate funds. An inscription from the ancient Greek historian Herodotus on the New York City post office states that nothing will stymie or hold back the delivery of mail: "Neither snow, nor rain, nor heat, nor gloom of night stays these couriers [i.e., the Persian pony express] from the swift completion of their appointed rounds."

Synonyms: block, hinder, frustrate, stump, confuse, baffle, perplex, bewilder, thwart (THWORT)

Related words: confound, impede, obstruct, hamper, nonplus

Working With Words

I. Fill in each blank with the appropriate word from the following list:

penitently	urbane
admonished	nonchalantly
iridescent	stymied
cajoled	accolades
paradoxically	banal

Each word must be used only once.

While I was anxiously preparing for my first date, my grandmother seated me beside her and (1)___*admonished*___ me to be careful about young men. She told me how as a young country girl working in her father's general store she met a traveling salesman. Unlike the youths in her small town who seemed crude, bumbling, and unsophisticated, this young salesman appeared refined, elegant, and (2)___*urbane*___. My grandmother had never before been alone with a boy on a date, but the salesman's smooth talk (3)___*cajoled*___ her into going with him to a local movie. The film portrayed the career of a young farm girl who left for the big city, rose to cinema stardom, and received the highest (4)___*accolades*___, including an Academy Award. Grandmother was overwhelmed by the story and imagined herself parading in the actress' brilliant, colorful, (5)___*iridescent*___ costumes. After the film, my grandmother's companion invited her to the most expensive restaurant in town. He asked if she would care for a drink; she tried to give the appearance of (6)___*nonchalantly*___ accepting, although she had never before tasted alcohol. Reacting to the drink, she chattered about the most ordinary, pointless, (7)___*banal*___ incidents of her life. (8)___*Paradoxically*___, her commonplace remarks impressed him more than any witty, sophisticated, brilliant conversation ever could.

He then drove her to her home, said he had a wonderful time, and wished her good night. My grandmother murmured some confusing reply and returned to her room. She began feeling guilty about the date and (9)___*penitently*___ vowed never to see the man again. When he appeared in her father's store the next day, she was utterly confused, perplexed, (10)___*stymied*___. To make a long story short, he declared his love for her and soon after they were married. What had begun as an admonishment by my grandmother about the dangers of dating turned into a romantic story about how she met grandfather—such are the paradoxes of life.

II. Match the word on the left with its synonyms.

____1. banal	a. reprove, warn
____2. urbane	b. Catch-22, contradiction
____3. cajole	c. thwart, block
____4. paradox	d. insipid, unimaginative
____5. admonish	e. lustrous, colorful
____6. penitent	f. coax, persuade
____7. iridescent	g. contrite, sorry
____8. nonchalant	h. laurels, honor
____9. stymie	i. suave, sophisticated
___10. accolade	j. insouciant, carefree

III. Word Part: CED—go, yield (precede)

recede (rih SEED) *v.* move backward; slope or slant backward

secede (sih SEED) *v.* withdraw formally from membership, especially from a political or religious association

intercede (in tur SEED) *v.* ask or plead for another; help settle a dispute or bring about an agreement between differing parties

concede (kon SEED) *v.* grant or admit as true or right; yield, give up

precedent (PRES ih dunt) *n.* something said or done earlier that serves
as an example or justification

***Using each of the five CED words only once, complete the following
sentences.***

1. If you ___Secede___ from our organization, we will never take
you back.

2. I don't need anyone to ___intercede___ for me with the school
principal; I will explain the situation to him myself.

3. As the years proceed, our hairlines ___recede___.

4. He reasoned so carefully that even his worst enemy would have to
___concede___ that he was right.

5. Although the United States has never had a woman President, other
countries—such as Israel, India, and England—can serve as a
___precedent___ that women can be national leaders.

Chapter 9

1. recalcitrant	6. tally
2. pinnacle	7. bizarre
3. siren	8. remorse
4. Adonis	9. spurious
5. inexorable	10. fervent

1. *recalcitrant* (rih KAL sih trunt) *adj.*   stubbornly resisting authority, discipline, guidance, or treatment

This word kicks like a stubborn mule. "Recalcitrant" derives from Latin *recalcitrare* (*re* = "back," *calcitrare* = "kick") which literally applied to the defiant kicking back of an unmanageable horse or mule. A contemporary of Charles Dickens, fellow novelist William Thackery—best known for *Vanity Fair*—introduced the word into English.

Even if they don't kick, recalcitrant children still plague babysitters and teachers. In Shakespeare's *The Taming of the Shrew*, the hero Petruchio tames his unruly wife, the recalcitrant Kate. Rather than comply with the Supreme Court decision to integrate schools, Arkansas Governor Orval Faubus recalcitrantly closed the high schools of Little Rock in 1958.

Synonyms: unruly, undisciplined, unmanageable, rebellious, disobedient, defiant, obstinate, refractory (rih FRAK tuh ree)

Related words: intractable, contumacious

Contracted words: amenable, tractable, docile, compliant, submissive

2. *pinnacle* (PIN uh KUL) *n.* highest point

From approximately 500 B.C. until the 1800's, writers used pens made from feathers. Appropriately, "pen" comes from Latin *penna* for "feather" or "wing." Similarly, "pinnacle" from Latin *pinna* (an alternate form of *penna*) signified a small wing-like projection above the tower or roof of a building. Hence, "pinnacle" came to mean the highest point, either physically as in a mountain peak or metaphorically as in the summit or peak of one's success. In 1776 Thomas Jefferson penned one of the pinnacles of Western democracy—the Declaration of Independence.

Synonyms: peak, summit, climax, acme (AK mee)

Related words: zenith, culmination, apogee, apex

Contrasted words: nadir, nethermost point

3. *siren* (SY run) *n.* beautiful and dangerously fascinating woman who attracts and tempts men

The song of the Sirens lured men to their death. From their island, these Sirens or bird-women would attract passing ships with sweet melodies and alluring words that no human could resist. Forsaking their ships, sailors would swim to the Siren's island, spending the rest of their lives captivated by song. Greek mythology tells of how Odysseus—the Greek hero who conceived of the Trojan Horse that enabled the Greeks to conquer Troy—heard this music and lived. Approaching the island of the Sirens, Odysseus ordered his men to place wax in their ears and then securely bind him to the mast of the ship. Deaf to the Siren's songs, the crew safely maneuvered the ship past the island while Odysseus, frantically but unsuccessfully struggling to break his bonds, heard the enchanting melodies. From these Sirens came English "siren," meaning both a device producing a loud warning signal and a dangerously attractive woman. "Siren" may also be used as an adjective, as when corporations lure talented employees with siren songs of irresistibly high salaries and enticing fringe benefits.

Hollywood screen siren Marilyn Monroe married baseball great

Joe DiMaggio and later playwright Arthur Miller, author of *Death of a Salesman* and *The Crucible*. Although no campus siren could distract him from his studies, the bookworm—a devoted fan of writer Kurt Vonnegut, Jr.—could not resist putting aside his homework to read the author's science fiction novel *The Sirens of Titan*. Synonymous with "siren," "femme fatale"—from French *fatale* ("fatal," "dangerous") and *femme* ("woman")—was first recorded in a 1912 letter of Britain's greatest dramatist since Shakespeare, George Bernard Shaw: "I saw a *Femme Fatale* who was a fine figure of a woman."

Synonyms: tempting woman, charmer, seductress, femme fatale (fem fuh TAL)

Related words: temptress, enchantress

4. *Adonis* (uh DON ihs) *n.* extremely handsome young man

Even the goddess of love, called Aphrodite by the Greeks and Venus by the Romans, could herself fall in love. The object of her passion, a beautiful youth named Adonis, delighted in hunting. Venus warned him to chase only small game, but one day Adonis pursued a fierce, wild boar. The youth hurled his spear but merely wounded the beast. Enraged, the huge-tusked boar fatally gored Adonis. Venus caused a lovely red flower—the anemone or windflower —to sprout from her lover's blood. Shakespeare gave his version of this affair in his long narrative poem *Venus and Adonis*. Today, we may refer to an exceptionally handsome lifeguard, singer, or actor as an Adonis.

Another strikingly handsome figure from Greek mythology was Apollo—god of light, music, and medicine. Like Venus, Apollo fell in love with a beautiful youth who was fated for early death. During a playful discus-throwing contest between the god and his beloved companion, Apollo's discus accidentally struck the youth in the forehead. From the blood of Apollo's lost love Hyacinth bloomed the flower bearing the youth's name.

Though radiantly handsome, Apollo often suffered disastrous love affairs. He feel in love with Cassandra, a princess of Troy. To win her affection, Apollo gave her the gift of prophecy. Cassandra still rejected the advances of the god. Angered and unable to take back his gift—gods could not reclaim what they had once granted—Apollo caused her prophecies to be always disbelieved. Cassandra's fellow Trojans ignored her warning not to admit the gigantic wooden horse that secretly housed the enemy Greeks. Hence, today a Cassandra is a person whose warnings of approaching evil are disregarded.

Although "Adonis" is used more often than "Apollo" to refer to extraordinarily handsome men, Apollo Creed—the heavyweight champion dethroned by Rocky in the film series *Rocky*—evidently chose his name to emphasize what he considered to be his beautiful, Greek-god appearance.

Synonyms: handsome man, matinee ideal, "hunk" (slang), Apollo (uh POL oh)

5. *inexorable* (in EK sur uh bul) *adj.* unchangeable or unstoppable by pleading or begging; unyielding

For some people prayer is a last resort. If their prayers cannot change events, these events must inexorably occur. "Inexorable" stems from Latin *in* ("not") + *ex* ("out") + *orare* ("pray," "speak"); we cannot speak or pray our way out of what is inexorable or unalterable. There can be no agreement between workers inexorable in their demands for increased pay and a boss who is inexorably opposed to those demands. The oracles (similarly derived from *orare*) of ancient Greece could be either the sacred places where visitors sought the prophecies of the gods or the priests who transmitted these prophecies. The prophecies were often deliberately vague, capable of more than one interpretation. According to the ancient Greek historian Herodotus, the fabulously wealthy monarch Croesus visited the most famous of all oracles—the oracle at Delphi, sacred to the god Apollo. Croesus asked if he should attack the Persians. The oracle answered that if Croesus attacked, he would destroy a great empire. Croesus then attacked the Persians. Unfortunately, he lost, so that the empire he destroyed was his own. Though Croesus did not realize it at the time, the oracle's prophecy concerned Croesus's own inexorable doom. Inexorably fated for defeat, Croesus had no chance for victory.

Synonyms: inflexible, rigid, unbending, inescapable, relentless (rih LENT less)

Related words: unrelenting, adamant, obdurate, resolute, intractable

Contrasted words: compliant, pliable, pliant, tractable, lenient

6. *tally* (TAL ee) *v.* count up, add, record

Long before the days of the computer, people calculated with sticks and stones. "Calculate" itself derives from *calculus*, the Latin word for the little stones or pebbles that helped the Romans to add and subtract. An ancient method of reckoning loans was to take a piece of wood, notch it with the amount of the loan, then split the wood lengthwise. Lender and borrower each kept a half. When it came time to repay the loan, the matching of the halves confirmed the transaction. Up until the nineteenth century, the English government recorded loans with these wooden pieces called "tallies" or "Tally sticks" (ultimately from Latin *talea*—"cutting," "rod," "stick"). Curiously, corporations and governments now issue stocks ("stock" deriving from Germanic *stock* meaning "stick") instead of sticks. I hope this account isn't too sticky to understand.

Hence, when we tally votes, we add them up to see who wins an election. "Tally" also means "match," "agree," "correspond," as when parents get upset because their child's report card doesn't tally with the student's stories of academic success. In addition to being a verb, "tally" functions as a noun when we examine the tally or account of business transactions.

Synonyms: register, count, compute, calculate, tabulate (TAB yuh late)

Related word: enumerate

7. *bizarre* (bih ZAHR) *adj.* very strange, odd, fantastic

Etymologists usually trace "bizarre" to French *bizarre* ("odd," "fantastic"), ultimately deriving from Italian *bizzarro* ("angry"). However, there is an old story that "bizarre" comes from the Basque word *bizar* for "beard." Unrelated to any other known language, Basque is the language of an ancient people inhabiting southern France and northern Spain around the mountainous Pyrenees border. Presumably, the Basques thought their beards handsome, but the French thought the Basque beards peculiar. Hence, the French referred to the strange-looking bearded Basques as "bizarre," and eventually the word acquired the general meaning of "odd" or "fantastic." Many etymologists nowadays think this story too bizarre to be true.

"Grotesque," similar in meaning to "bizarre," derives from Italian *grotta* ("cave"). Archaeologists unearthed caves containing ancient Roman statues and murals. These art works represented fantastic combinations of animals, humans, and exotic vegetation. Because of its association with strange visual representations, *grotta* evolved into our word "grotesque," referring to anything odd, distorted, deformed, ridiculous, repulsive, or absurd.

Synonyms: unusual, weird, queer, freakish, grotesque (gro TESK)

Related words: outlandish, eccentric, abnormal, ludicrous

Contrasted words: inconspicuous, subdued

8. *remorse* (rih MORS) *n.* bitter and painful sense of guilt

When we feel we are being eaten away by sorrow and regret for some past action, we are suffering remorse. The sense of being eaten or gnawed at can be seen in the Latin source of "remorse," *re* ("again") + *mordere* ("bite"). "Morsel" or "tiny bit of food" has the same source. Dieters who can't resist some sweet high-calorie morsel often suffer remorse. Remorseful criminals may volunteer to work without pay for their victims. After the prophet Nathan admonished King David for gaining Bathsheba by killing her husband, David remorsefully prayed for forgiveness. When the Greek hero Odysseus returned home from the Trojan War after twenty years to find his house plagued by men eating his food, molesting his servants, and desiring to marry his wife, he slew those men without remorse. "Remorseless" means "without pity or mercy." In Herman Melville's *Moby Dick*, the vengeful Captain Ahab remorselessly pursues the white whale that chewed off and made a morsel of his leg.

Synonyms: regret, guilt, compunction (kum PUNGK shun)

Related words: contrition, penitence, repentance, self-reproach, qualm, rue, ruefulness

9. *spurious* (SPYOOR [rhymes with first syllable of "furious"] ee us) *adj.* not genuine

You might say that "spurious" was born out of wedlock since Latin *spurius* meant "illegitimate child." "Spurious" first entered English referring to illegitimate birth, then was extended to describe anything of illegitimate or irregular origin, and finally came to have the general meaning of "false," "fake," "counterfeit." Courts are plagued by spurious wills, museums by spurious art works, immigration officials by spurious passports, and insurance companies by spurious claims. In Shakespeare's *King Lear*, the illegitimate or bastard son Edmund counterfeits a letter in his brother's handwriting stating a desire to kill their father. By revealing this spurious letter to their father, Edmund plans to get the legitimate Edgar's inheritance. Edmund soliloquizes or speaks his thoughts aloud to the audience:

> Well then,
> Legitimate Edgar, I must have your land.
> Our father's love is to the bastard Edmund
> As to the legitimate. Fine word, "legitimate."
> Well, my legitimate, if this letter speed,
> And my invention [plot] thrive, Edmund the base
> Shall top the legitimate. I grow, I prosper.
> Now, gods, stand up for bastards.

Mark Twain revealed the spuriousness of a death notice with this cable to the Associated Press: "The reports of my death have been greatly exaggerated."

Synonyms: false, counterfeit, fake, apocryphal (uh POK ruh ful)

Related words: inauthentic, unauthentic, fraudulent, fallacious, sham, ersatz

Contrasted words: authentic, bona fide, veracious

10. *fervent* (FUR vunt) *adj.* intense, passionate

> Double, double, toil and trouble,
> Fire burn and cauldron bubble.

The three witches in Shakespeare's *Macbeth* chant this refrain as they boil some devilish brew. You might say that they are fervently at work in more than one sense. In the modern sense of "fervent," they are intense and earnest in their task; since "fervent" derives from Latin *fervere* ("boil") and is linguistically related to "brew," the etymological overtones of "fervent" also particularly suit the supernatural cooks and their fiendish stew. Today, "fervent" remains hot in the sense of passionate, as when we fervently support a cause, give a fervent speech, or are fervent admirers. "Fervid" has the same etymology and is synonymous with "fervent." Another hot word is "ardent," from Latin *ardere* ("burn"). Also synonymous with "fervent," "ardent" can suggest romance, as when we describe Romeo and Juliet as ardent lovers. Although we may work intensely with ardor and fervor, don't confuse "ardor" with "arduous" (meaning "difficult," "strenuous"). Of course, someone filled with ardor or passion may still have to labor arduously, for as Shakespeare puts it in *A Midsummer Night's Dream*, "The course of true love never did run smooth."

Synonyms: earnest, enthusiastic, spirited, fiery, ardent (AHR [pronounced like the letter "r"] dunt)

Related words: impassioned, zealous, vehement

Contrasted words: apathetic, phlegmatic, dispassionate, impassive, indifferent, aloof

Working With Words

I. Fill in each blank with the appropriate word from the following list:

pinnacle
fervently
tallied
bizarre
recalcitrant

Adonis
spurious
remorse
siren
inexorable

Each word must be used only once.

An unruly, rebellious, (1)___recalcitrant___ child, John Steele had trouble conforming to school authorities and, upon graduating from high school, found it equally difficult to meet the demands of his employers. Blessed with extraordinary good looks—he was, indeed, an (2)___Adonis___—John left for Hollywood and became an actor. After several small parts, he worked in a film with a famous actress noted for her sexy, seductive roles. Off screen, however, this actress proved to be no destructive temptress or (3)___siren___ luring men to their destruction but a dedicated, disciplined performer who was committed to her profession and compassionately guided young performers. John and the actress became close friends. Under her direction, the once recalcitrant student now strove (4)___fervently___ to master his craft. He learned how a subtle gesture, the length of a pause, a slight change of tone could either make an emotion seem real and genuine or fake and (5)___spurious___. He carefully (6)___tallied___ his strengths and weaknesses so as to profit from the former and eliminate the latter. John became his own severest taskmaster, never content until he met his own unyielding, (7)___inexorable___ demands for performances of the highest quality. Success rapidly followed, and John Steele soon reached the (8)___pinnacle___ of his profession. In a (9)___bizarre___ turn of events, John Steele—one-time unruly and recalcitrant pupil—now visits schools to encourage students to work their hardest and pursue their dreams with fervent self-discipline. Only by inexorably following this route, he counsels, will one eventually be able to find self-fulfillment and avoid the (10)___remorse___ that accompanies neglected talent, missed opportunities, and a wasted life.

II. Match the word on the left with its synonyms.

____1. pinnacle	a. tabulate, count
____2. remorse	b. apocryphal, false
____3. tally	c. acme, peak
____4. recalcitrant	d. compunction, regret
____5. Adonis	e. refractory, disobedient
____6. fervent	f. grotesque, weird
____7. siren	g. Apollo, handsome man
____8. spurious	h. femme fatale, seductress
____9. bizarre	i. relentless, unyielding
___10. inexorable	j. ardent, intense

III. Word Part: CAPIT—head (capital, capitol)

capitulate (kuh PITCH uh late) *v.* surrender, give up

recapitulate (ree kuh PITCH uh late) *v.*   summarize

decapitate (dih KAP uh tate) *v.* cut off the head, behead

per capita (pur KAP uh tuh) *adj. or adv.* for each person (of population): per person

capitalize (KAP uh tuh lize) *v.* take advantage of or profit from (when "capitalize" has this meaning, it is always followed by "on")

Using each of the five CAPIT words only once, complete the following sentences.

1. Health experts worry about the high ___per capita___ consumption of sugar and salt.

2. We asked the teacher to ___re capitulate___ the main parts of her lecture so that we could summarize the essential ideas in our notes.

3. Skillful tennis players quickly ___capitalize___ on their opponents' mistakes.

4. The guillotine—the official execution instrument of the French Revolution—would behead or ___decapitate___ the victim.

5. When the British asked the Revolutionary War hero Captain John Paul Jones to surrender, he answered that he would never ___capitulate___: "I have not yet begun to fight."

Chapter 10

1. harbinger	6. meretricious
2. opportune	7. lampoon
3. skeptical	8. fetish
4. cardinal	9. zenith
5. trivial	10. nadir

1. *harbinger* (HAR bin jur) *n.* person or thing that signals what will follow

"Harbinger" is an old war word, ultimately coming from German *heri* ("army") + *berga* ("shelter"). The earliest harbingers were hosts providing lodgings for an army. Later, the harbingers were the army scouts who sought shelter for the rest of the troops. Gradually, the harbinger lost his military association and came to be anyone seeking room and board for a group of travelers. Finally, "harbinger" assumed the general meaning of an "announcer of things to come."

Dark clouds, lightning, and thunder are harbingers of an approaching storm. In his epic poem *Paradise Lost*, John Milton called Venus "the evening star, Love's harbinger." Near the end of Shakespeare's *Macbeth*, Macduff signals the battle that will destroy Macbeth:

> Make all trumpets speak, give them all breath,
> Those clamorous harbingers of blood and death.

Legend has it that if on February 2 the groundhog or woodchuck sees its shadow there will be six more weeks of winter weather; if it doesn't see its shadow, then the groundhog is a harbinger of spring weather soon to come.

Synonyms: forerunner, herald, announcer, precursor (prih KUR sur)

2. *opportune* (op ur TOON) *adj.* timely, suitable, favorable

Ancient Romans held an annual feast honoring Portunus, the god who protected harbors and ports. "Opportune" still pays homage to this deity, for the word derives from *ob* ("before") + *portus* ("port"), the favorable time when ships were safely in the harbor. Now we regard any fitting or appropriate time as opportune.

It would have been opportune to invest in IBM and Sony when those corporations first formed. Alone at last with the girl of his dreams, the young man found the moment opportune to declare his love.

Synonyms: well-timed, appropriate, convenient, auspicious (aw SPISH us)

Related words: propitious, advantageous, apt, felicitous

Contrasted word: inopportune

3. *skeptical* (SKEP tih kul) *adj.* doubting, questioning

In ancient Greece, the Skeptics were a group of philosophers who believed that we cannot be sure that our observations correspond to the real world. They argued that there is no way of proving that our observations are not the result of a hallucination, mirage, or dream. Thus they doubted that we can ever accurately know the world outside of our minds. The Scottish philosopher David Hume (1711-1776) is famous as a great skeptic. He even doubted that we can know for sure whether anything causes anything else. We may observe that every time one billiard ball hits another billiard ball, the second billiard ball moves. Hume would argue, however, that our impression that one billiard ball necessarily causes another billiard ball to move is based on a series of observations that psychologically condition us to expect this reaction.

Since one ball striking another has always seemingly caused the second ball to move in the past, we become mentally conditioned to think that this reaction will always occur. However, Hume would say that there is no logical necessity that the reaction will always happen. For example, just because a dog has been rewarded with food every time it jumps through a hoop does not necessarily mean that the dog will always get food after it leaps. The dog has been psychologically conditioned to think that its jump will inevitably cause a reward of food. Whereas we can see the dog's mistake (since the trainer could easily withhold the food), Hume claims that we make the same mistake in thinking that one thing necessarily causes another. We may not be as skeptical as the Greek Skeptics or Hume, but we may be skeptical of advertisements that promise fifteen minutes a day of exercise will transform us into Miss or Mr. America. Many doctors at first skeptically sneered at Louis Pasteur's theory that microbes cause disease, but Pasteur proved the skeptics wrong.

Synonyms: disbelieving, doubtful, suspicious, incredulous (in KREJ uh lus)

Related words: dubious, cynical

Contrasted words: credulous, naive, gullible

4. *cardinal* (KAR duh nul) *adj.* fundamental, chief, of basic importance

Several meanings hinge on the word "cardinal," which appropriately derives from Latin *cardo* ("hinge"). A door hinge is of central importance since the door depends upon it to pivot or swing. Metaphorically, *cardinalis* ("pertaining to a hinge") referred to that on which anything depends, in other words, something of crucial importance. Church cardinals acquired their name because of their high office. Since the cardinals wore deep-red robes, the color of these robes came to be called "cardinal." The bird "cardinal" acquired its name because its bright red feathers resembled the church cardinal's robes. We could go on to explain the origin of the cardinal numbers (one, two, three, etc. in contrast to the ordinal numbers first, second, third, etc.) and the cardinal virtues of justice, prudence temperance and fortitude as opposed to the seven deadly sins (wrath, avarice, sloth, pride, lust, envy, gluttony),but your cardinal concern may be to take a break from etymology—so relax and enjoy some entertainment, perhaps a baseball game with the St. Louis Cardinals.

Synonyms: main, central, essential, principal, paramount (PAR uh mount)

Related words: prime, primary, preeminent

Contrasted words: subordinate, trivial, inconsequential, negligible

5. *trivial* (TRIV ee ul) *adj.* of little importance

"Trivial" derives from Latin *tri* ("three") and *via* ("road"). At a *trivium* ("place where three roads met"), Romans often engaged in small talk, gossip, and idle conversation—in other words, the same insignificant chatter that we still hear at our street corners. The triple intersection was often the site of a market where people leisurely chatted. From its association with commonplace talk, "trivial" acquired its meaning of "unimportant."

An old Buddhist story tells of how a monk arrived at a river and waited for a ferry. A second monk, who had a great reputation for holiness, came along and proceeded to walk across the surface of the water and then returned to the first monk. Rather than being overwhelmed with the feat of the second monk, the first monk said, "What is so great about walking on water to get to the other side of the river? For a few pennies I could ferry across." Evidently, the first monk thought that spiritual growth meant more than supernatural feats. He regarded the second monk's demonstration as trivial rather than spiritual.

Synonyms: unimportant, ordinary, commonplace, insignificant, inconsequential (in kon suh KWEN shul)

Related words: paltry, petty, negligible, trifling, nugatory, picayune

Contrasted words: consequential, momentous, vital, crucial

6. *meretricious* (mer uh TRISH us)   *adj.*   insincere; vulgarly, showily, or cheaply attractive

Since Genesis which portrayed Eve as the persuasive cause of Adam's downfall, women have been abused in literature and language. Sexism functions in the etymology of "meretricious," derived from Latin *merere* ("earn pay"). Positively, *merere* evolved into our "merit," from the implication of a man's being paid for an honest day's labor. Negatively, *merere* led to the Latin word for "prostitute" *meretrix*—literally a "female earner of pay" as *trix* is a feminine forming suffix—and ultimately to our word "meretricious," the implication being that a woman's earnings came about dishonestly. Originally, "meretricious" meant "pertaining to a prostitute," as when Shakespeare's contemporary Francis Bacon wrote, "The Delight in Meretricious Embracements (where sin is turned into Art) maketh Marriage a dull thing." Now "meretricious" refers to flashy, deceptive attractiveness. Someone may create a meretricious display of wealth by holding parties that are all tinsel and glitter, though that person is verging on bankruptcy. Concerned parents try to steer their children away from meretricious books and movies. Do not confuse "meretricious" with "meritorious." A student getting back a term paper with the teacher's comment "a meretricious effort" may unwittingly regard the comment as praise.

Synonyms: flashy, showy, tawdry (TAW drec)

Related words: gaudy, garish, specious, spurious

Contrasted words: authentic

7. *lampoon* (lam POON)   *n.*   ridiculous or humorous attack on a person, group, or institution

Drunken seventeenth-century French students would sing a *lampon*, an obscene, humorous, abusive song. These drinking songs (*lampons* = "guzzle," "gulp") often made fun of their subjects. Today, "lampoon" refers to an attack that may range from lighthearted humor to vicious ridicule. Lampoons of political humorists mock government officials and policies. "Lampoon" is both noun and verb, as when Harvard students lampoon their victims in the students' appropriately named publication—*Harvard Lampoon.*

Synonyms: mockery, ridicule, satire (SA tire)

Related words: travesty, burlesque, parody, farce, caricature, invective

8. *fetish* (FET ish) *n.* object of obsessive concern or unreasoning devotion

Early Portuguese voyagers to Guinea on the western coast of Africa found the Africans worshipping small objects that presumably had the power to work good or evil. The Portuguese called these charms *feitico*. Our word "fetish," derived from *feitico*, still carries the meaning of an "object worshipped for its magical powers." However, we more often use "fetish" in the broader sense of an "object of unquestioning or irrational devotion."

   Dieters make a fetish of counting calories. Cleanliness may be next to godliness, but some individuals make such a fetish of cleaning that they will rage over a loose thread in a rug, a book unevenly positioned on its shelf, or a particle of dust on the bureau. Critics of U.S. culture say that America's concern with leisure, youthful appearance, and material success amounts to a fetish. The psychological sense of "fetish" refers to a normally nonsexual object such as a foot or glove that arouses erotic feelings.

Synonyms: passion, obsession, mania (MAY nee uh)

Related words: preoccupation, penchant, fixation, amulet, talisman

9. *zenith* (ZEE nith) *n.* point in the sky directly overhead; highest point

10. *nadir* (NAY dur) *n.* point in the sky directly opposite the zenith and directly beneath the observer; lowest point

During the Middle Ages, the Arab world surpassed Europe in science. Our word "algebra" comes from the Arabs who helped develop this branch of mathematics. Whereas medieval European astronomy stagnated, the Arabs of this period carefully observed the heavens. "Zenith" and "nadir" derive from Arabic astronomical terms. The Arabic word *samt*—from the phrase *samt arras* ("way over the head")—had a variant *semt*. Some etymologists theorize that a European copier of texts mistook the "m" in *semt* for "ni" and rendered the word into medieval Latin as *cenit*. Eventually, the word entered English as *senyth*, which became "zenith." "Nadir" comes from Arabic *nazir* ("opposite"), referring to the point in the sky that is directly opposite the zenith.

Jesse Owens reached the highest point or zenith of his athletic career when he won four gold medals at the Berlin Olympics in 1936. Ulysses S. Grant rose from the nadir of his career in the 1850's—when he failed as a farmer, rental agent, and U.S. Customs House official—to his zenith in the 1860's as victorious Union general, national hero, and President.

Synonyms for "zenith": peak, climax, summit, apex (A [pronounced like the letter "a"] pex)

Related words for "zenith": culmination, pinnacle, acme, apogee

Synonyms for "nadir": low point, depths, bottom, nethermost (NETH ur most) point

Working With Words

I. Fill in each blank with the appropriate word from the following list:

nadir	opportune
cardinal	zenith
meretricious	trivial
lampoon	skeptical
harbinger	fetish

Each word must be used only once.

Perhaps the most famous poem about baseball is Ernest Lawrence Thayer's "Casey at the Bat." The poem opens with Mudville, the home team, trailing two to four with two outs in the last half of the ninth inning. A few of the local fans begin to straggle from the park, for two of the poorest hitters are up next, one of them described as a cheap, flashy, (1)_____ fake. To everyone's surprise, these two ballplayers get hits. Up steps Casey, the mightiest slugger on the team. With two men on base and the Mudville hero at bat, the crowd senses that the favorable or (2)_____ moment has arrived. To the screaming multitude, Casey is the (3)_____ of victory. So great is the fans' confidence in their champion, that no one remains doubtful or (4)_____ that Mudville will emerge triumphant. Casey ceremoniously enacts the hitter's obsessive concern or (5)_____ of rubbing his hands with dirt and wiping them on his shirt. When the umpire calls the first pitch a strike, the crowd threatens to kill him, but Casey shrugs off the call as unimportant or (6)_____ and raises his hand to silence his supporters. But when the umpire also calls the second pitch a strike, everyone realizes that the next pitch will be of (7)_____ importance. Casey will either soar to the (8)_____ of his career or sink to its (9)_____. With lines that some read with sorrow and others with humor—although no baseball devotee could ever consider the verse as merely ridiculous satire or (10)_____—the poem concludes:

Oh, somewhere in this favored land the sun is shining bright,
The band is playing somewhere, and somewhere hearts are
   light;
And somewhere men are laughing, and somewhere children
   shout,
But there is no joy in Mudville—Mighty Casey has struck out.

II. Match the word on the left with its synonym.

____1. cardinal   a. auspicious, favorable

____2. fetish   b. tawdry, cheaply attractive

____3. meretricious   c. precursor, herald

____4. skeptical   d. mania, obsession

____5. lampoon   e. incredulous, suspicious

____6. nadir   f. satire, ridicule

____7. trivial   g. paramount, essential

____8. zenith   h. inconsequential, unimportant

____9. opportune   i. nethermost point, lowpoint

___10. harbinger   j. apex, peak

III. Word Part: LUD—play (ludicrous)

elude (ih LOOD) *v.* escape, avoid, slip away

delude (dih LOOD) *v.* mislead, fool, deceive

allude (uh LOOD) *v.* refer indirectly, mention casually

prelude (PREL yood) *n.* introductory act, event, performance or musical piece; introduction

interlude (IN tur lood) *n.* something that comes between two events

Using each of the five LUD words only once, complete the following sentences.

1. Although we openly criticized the boss behind her back, no one dared to _____ to her faults in her presence.

2. The first snowflake was a _____ to a white Christmas.

3. Between rounds in a boxing match, there is a one-minute _____ of rest.

4. We often _____ ourselves rather than seeing things as they really are.

5. The crafty fox managed to _____ all of our traps and escaped to freedom.

MASTER EXERCISES

Select the definition closest in meaning in the following exercises.

I. This exercise reviews all words with a story.

1. **abominable**
   (a) pleasant
   (b) disgusting
   (c) cautious
   (d) explosive

2. **Achilles' heel**
   (a) bum
   (b) warrior
   (c) weakness
   (d) strength

3. **accolade**
   (a) castle
   (b) humor
   (c) sadness
   (d) honor

4. **adamant**
   (a) unyielding
   (b) angry
   (c) pleasant
   (d) disgusting

5. **Adonis**
   (a) soldier
   (b) monster
   (c) coward
   (d) handsome man

6. **admonish**
   (a) warn
   (b) prevent
   (c) accuse
   (d) praise

7. **alleviate**
   (a) torture
   (b) relieve
   (c) depart
   (d) challenge

8. **anachronism**
   (a) dinosaur
   (b) patient
   (c) clown
   (d) time error

9. **asinine**
   (a) medicine
   (b) beverage
   (c) stupid
   (d) wise

10. **bacchanal**
    (a) wild party
    (b) religious retreat
    (c) vacation
    (d) examination

11. **banal**
    (a) hungry
    (b) satisfied
    (c) clever
    (d) ordinary

12. **bellwether**
    (a) leader
    (b) storm
    (c) roof
    (d) orchestra

13. **bizarre**   (a) market   (b) strange
                    (c) commonplace   (d) merchandise

14. **bombast**   (a) wordiness   (b) explosion
                    (c) earthquake   (d) disease

15. **cajole**   (a) persuade   (b) capture
                    (c) attack   (d) swallow

16. **cardinal**   (a) victorious   (b) defeated
                    (c) sweet   (d) essential

17. **charlatan**   (a) leader   (b) teacher
                    (c) swindler   (d) servant

18. **chimerical** (a) unrealistic   (b) practical
                    (c) sharp   (d) dull

19. **choleric**   (a) grouchy   (b) sad
                    (c) happy   (d) lazy

20. **cliché**   (a) truth   (b) falsehood
                    (c) wealth   (d) stale expression

21. **conjugal**   (a) harmonious   (b) bitter
                    (c) married   (d) secure

22. **despotic**   (a) friendly   (b) reasonable
                    (c) crazy   (d) tyrannical

23. **desultory**   (a) serious   (b) funny
                    (c) aimless   (d) harmful

24. **diabolic**   (a) evil   (b) kind
                    (c) powerful   (d) wise

25. **diatribe**   (a) support   (b) enthusiasm
                    (c) opponent   (d) verbal attack

26. **disparage**   (a) dive   (b) drown
                    (c) fly   (d) degrade

27. **draconian**
(a) mild
(b) casy
(c) swift
(d) harsh

28. **dunce**
(a) fool
(b) teacher
(c) manager
(d) toy

29. **effete**
(a) splendid
(b) unproductive
(c) clever
(d) misleading

30. **esoteric**
(a) mysterious
(b) ordinary
(c) large
(d) ugly

31. **exonerate**
(a) punish
(b) blame
(c) free
(d) help

32. **farce**
(a) mockery
(b) honor
(c) thief
(d) victim

33. **fatal**
(a) pleasant
(b) serious
(c) innocent
(d) deadly

34. **fathom**
(a) hit
(b) inform
(c) understand
(d) destroy

35. **fervent**
(a) intense
(b) sluggish
(c) sick
(d) healthy

36. **fetish**
(a) nightmare
(b) joke
(c) obsession
(d) answer

37. **gadfly**
(a) critic
(b) shield
(c) monster
(d) soldier

38. **guile**
(a) confidence
(b) worship
(c) treachery
(d) bitterness

39. **gullible**
(a) trustful
(b) modest
(c) gigantic
(d) forceful

40. **harbinger**
(a) ruler
(b) climax
(c) loss
(d) announcer

41. **hedonist**　　(a) traveler　　　　(b) tyrant
　　　　　　　　　　(c) comedian　　　　(d) playboy

42. **hyperbole**　　(a) conflict　　　　(b) luxury
　　　　　　　　　　(c) protection　　　 (d) overstatement

43. **homage**　　　(a) nutrition　　　 (b) excitement
　　　　　　　　　　(c) respect　　　　　(d) poverty

44. **impecunious**　(a) poor　　　　　 (b) irritable
　　　　　　　　　　(c) bold　　　　　　(d) timid

45. **inexorable**　　(a) sick　　　　　 (b) healthy
　　　　　　　　　　(c) unyielding　　　 (d) flexible

46. **iridescent**　　(a) dull　　　　　 (b) colorful
　　　　　　　　　　(c) humorous　　　　(d) radioactive

47. **irony**　　　　(a) strength　　　 (b) stimulation
　　　　　　　　　　(c) sweetness　　　 (d) mockery

48. **lampoon**　　 (a) ridicule　　　　(b) praise
　　　　　　　　　　(c) fire　　　　　　(d) brightness

49. **limbo**　　　 (a) death　　　　　 (b) in-between state
　　　　　　　　　　(c) paradise　　　　(d) inflexibility

50. **macabre**　　 (a) weird　　　　　(b) helpful
　　　　　　　　　　(c) pleasure　　　　(d) verbal blunder

51. **malapropism**　(a) disease　　　　(b) hatred
　　　　　　　　　　(c) pleasure　　　　(d) verbal blunder

52. **maverick**　　(a) magician　　　 (b) type of doctor
　　　　　　　　　　(c) warrior　　　　 (d) individualist

53. **melancholy**　(a) happy　　　　　(b) sad
　　　　　　　　　　(c) intelligent　　 (d) stupid

54. **meretricious**　(a) injurious　　　(b) praiseworthy
　　　　　　　　　　(c) forceful　　　　(d) insincere

55. **mnemonic**   (a) powerful   (b) assisting memory
                     (c) luxurious   (d) causing poverty

56. **nadir**   (a) climax   (b) lowest point
                     (c) damage   (d) brain cell

57. **nefarious**   (a) negative   (b) evil
                     (c) talkative   (d) calm

58. **nihilist**   (a) priest   (b) student
                     (c) healer   (d) disbeliever

59. **nonchalant**   (a) serious   (b) unconcerned
                     (c) intense   (d) energetic

60. **ominous**   (a) favorable   (b) threatening
                     (c) mocking   (d) respectful

61. **opportune**   (a) suitable   (b) unconscious
                     (c) expected   (d) unexpected

62. **paradox**   (a) insanity   (b) happiness
                     (c) pain   (d) contradiction

63. **pariah**   (a) soldier   (b) athlete
                     (c) outcast   (d) celebrity

64. **pecuniary**   (a) honest   (b) brave
                     (c) weak   (d) financial

65. **pedigree**   (a) animal   (b) ancestry
                     (c) farm tool   (d) fame

66. **penitent**   (a) sorry   (b) crazy
                     (c) happy   (d) skillful

67. **phlegmatic**   (a) sluggish   (b) boring
                     (c) sick   (d) excited

68. **pinnacle**   (a) flag   (b) symbol
                     (c) peak   (d) bottom

69. **pittance**   (a) pity   (b) sorrow
    (c) fortune   (d) small amount

70. **plagiarize**   (a) hypnotize   (b) tease
    (c) delight   (d) copy

71. **plummet**   (a) help   (b) congratulate
    (c) dive   (d) nourish

72. **pragmatic**   (a) serious   (b) clever
    (c) stubborn   (d) practical

73. **preposterous**   (a) clear   (b) absurd
    (c) confused   (d) previous

74. **recalcitrant**   (a) memorable   (b) disobedient
    (c) religious   (d) respectful

75. **remorse**   (a) victory   (b) joy
    (c) regret   (d) defeat

76. **sadistic**   (a) sorrowful   (b) heavy
    (c) kind   (d) cruel

77. **sanguine**   (a) cheerful   (b) sluggish
    (c) cautious   (d) aggressive

78. **serendipity**   (a) ability   (b) chance
    (c) agreement   (d) organization

79. **siren**   (a) nurse   (b) tempting woman
    (c) friend   (d) enemy

80. **skeptical**   (a) severe   (b) passionate
    (c) doubting   (d) supportive

81. **somnolent**   (a) immense   (b) dry
    (c) furious   (d) drowsy

82. **Spartan**   (a) quarrelsome   (b) special
    (c) severe   (d) surprising

83. **spurious**   (a) genuine   (b) smooth
    (c) rough   (d) false

84. **spurn**   (a) accept   (b) reject
    (c) increase   (d) explain

85. **stentorian**   (a) flexible   (b) savage
    (c) loud   (d) empty

86. **stymie**   (a) block   (b) move
    (c) speed up   (d) protect

87. **sycophant**   (a) commander   (b) technician
    (c) rebel   (d) flunky

88. **tally**   (a) calculate   (b) surprise
    (c) whip   (d) complain

89. **tawdry**   (a) terrible   (b) soothing
    (c) vulgar   (d) supreme

90. **titanic**   (a) irritable   (b) unconscious
    (c) pleasant   (d) gigantic

91. **tribulation**   (a) suffering   (b) revolution
    (c) prevention   (d) progress

92. **trite**   (a) warm   (b) commonplace
    (c) original   (d) horrible

93. **trivial**   (a) unimportant   (b) truthful
    (c) divided   (d) carefree

94. **undermine**   (a) support   (b) weaken
    (c) flee   (d) catch

95. **urbane**   (a) crowded   (b) rapid
    (c) daring   (d) sophisticated

96. **vegetate**   (a) prevent   (b) think
    (c) be idle   (d) be upset

97. **venerate**   (a) sicken   (b) respect
                          (c) improve   (d) sell

98. **vindicate**   (a) justify   (b) accuse
                          (c) teach   (d) lead

99. **vindictive**   (a) timid   (b) revengeful
                          (c) brave   (d) lonesome

100. **zenith**   (a) happiness   (b) pain
                          (c) peak   (d) fear

II. *This exercise reviews all the synonyms that were reinforced by exercises in the individual chapters.*

1. **absolve**
   (a) kill
   (b) dilute
   (c) accuse
   (d) clear

2. **abstruse**
   (a) difficult
   (b) easy
   (c) playful
   (d) disobedient

3. **acme**
   (a) irritation
   (b) highest point
   (c) ruler
   (d) lowest pain

4. **affliction**
   (a) example
   (b) industry
   (c) cooperation
   (d) hardship

5. **anarchist**
   (a) rebel
   (b) tourist
   (c) cheater
   (d) guide

6. **apex**
   (a) summit
   (b) bottom
   (c) wisdom
   (d) sorrow

7. **apocryphal**
   (a) true
   (b) false
   (c) unusual
   (d) ordinary

8. **Apollo**
   (a) scientist
   (b) tempting woman
   (c) parent
   (d) handsome man

9. **ardent**
   (a) helpful
   (b) intelligent
   (c) suspicious
   (d) enthusiastic

10. **auspicious**
   (a) favorable
   (b) pretty
   (c) flexible
   (d) strict

11. **austere**
   (a) severe
   (b) passionate
   (c) generous
   (d) disgusting

12. **belittle**
   (a) inspect
   (b) escape
   (c) downgrade
   (d) encourage

13. **burlesque**
   (a) mockery
   (b) award
   (c) destruction
   (d) observation

14. **Catch-22**
(a) monument
(b) effort
(c) medicine
(d) contradiction

15. **chronological error**
(a) time error
(b) substitute
(c) explosion
(d) poverty

16. **coax**
(a) complain
(b) deceive
(c) speed up
(d) persuade

17. **comprehend**
(a) sleep
(b) understand
(c) fight
(d) give up

18. **compunction**
(a) regret
(b) punishment
(c) pleasure
(d) argument

19. **contrite**
(a) sorry
(b) irritable
(c) exceptional
(d) late

20. **credulous**
(a) sensible
(b) rich
(c) offensive
(d) trustful

21. **decadent**
(a) explosive
(b) unproductive
(c) practical
(d) committed

22. **dictatorial**
(a) comforting
(b) domineering
(c) senseless
(d) suspicious

23. **dolt**
(a) mechanic
(b) mechanical tool
(c) baby horse
(d) fool

24. **duplicity**
(a) cooperation
(b) friendship
(c) deceit
(d) rebellion

25. **exculpate**
(a) trap
(b) dig up ruins
(c) surprise
(d) free from blame

26. **femme fatale**
(a) clown
(b) tempting woman
(c) accident
(d) handsome man

27. **foreboding**
(a) threatening
(b) complaining
(c) thinking
(d) lying

28. **fortuity**
 (a) wealth   (b) sickness
 (c) chance   (d) creativity

29. **gaudy**
 (a) flashy   (b) modesty
 (c) boastful   (d) steady

30. **genealogy**
 (a) war   (b) negotiation
 (c) contestant   (d) ancestry

31. **ghastly**
 (a) horrible   (b) luxurious
 (c) wasteful   (d) temperamental

32. **goad**
 (a) tower   (b) sin
 (c) blessing   (d) gadfly

33. **grandiloquence**
 (a) royalty   (b) sleepiness
 (c) wordiness   (d) excitement

34. **grotesque**
 (a) weird   (b) lovable
 (c) victorious   (d) gigantic

35. **hackneyed**
 (a) hurt   (b) stale
 (c) timid   (d) brilliant

36. **haphazard**
 (a) planned   (b) comforting
 (c) aimless   (d) lucky

37. **heinous**
 (a) hopeless   (b) wicked
 (c) sad   (d) unexpected

38. **hurtle**
 (a) plunge   (b) count
 (c) expect   (d) watch

39. **inane**
 (a) secret   (b) silly
 (c) clever   (d) magical

40. **inconsequential**
 (a) unimportant   (b) magnificent
 (c) greedy   (d) sensitive

41. **incredulous**
 (a) quick   (b) unbelieving
 (c) open   (d) serious

42. **indigent**   (a) quiet   (b) loud
                      (c) poor   (d) rich

43. **infernal**   (a) fiendish   (b) praiseworthy
                      (c) powerful   (d) dull

44. **insipid**   (a) playful   (b) uninteresting
                      (c) glorious   (d) suggestive

45. **insouciant**   (a) wicked   (b) threatening
                      (c) carefree   (d) confused

46. **irascible**   (a) calm   (b) easily angered
                      (c) complex   (d) simple

47. **laurels**   (a) honor   (b) odor
                      (c) discovery   (d) environment

48. **lethal**   (a) peculiar   (b) deadly
                      (c) careful   (d) lucky

49. **loathsome**   (a) disgusting   (b) attractive
                      (c) clever   (d) dull

50. **ludicrous**   (a) cautious   (b) bold
                      (c) stubborn   (d) ridiculous

51. **lustrous**   (a) smooth   (b) talkative
                      (c) brilliant   (d) cooperative

52. **mania**   (a) obsession   (b) splendor
                      (c) nonsense   (d) advice

53. **marital**   (a) aggressive   (b) pleasant
                      (c) married   (d) lost

54. **mitigate**   (a) memorize   (b) hasten
                      (c) perform   (d) relieve

55. **modicum**   (a) monster   (b) small amount
                      (c) pressure   (d) largest portion

56. **monetary**
    (a) poor   (b) loud
    (c) financial   (d) crooked

57. **mountebank**
    (a) swindler   (b) mechanic
    (c) explorer   (d) pleasure

58. **nethermost**
    (a) excited   (b) brave
    (c) lowest   (d) brilliant

59. **nonconformist**
    (a) servant   (b) laborer
    (c) follower   (d) individualist

60. **obdurate**
    (a) happy   (b) unyielding
    (c) new   (d) ancient

61. **oblivion**
    (a) pride   (b) anger
    (c) laziness   (d) neglect

62. **optimistic**
    (a) new   (b) practical
    (c) hopeful   (d) solid

63. **orgy**
    (a) diet   (b) wild party
    (c) calm mind   (d) vacation

64. **paramount**
    (a) essential   (b) unnecessary
    (c) empty   (d) loose

65. **persona non grata**
    (a) hero   (b) unacceptable person
    (c) celebrity   (d) tempting woman

66. **perversely cruel**
    (a) kind   (b) unintentionally cruel
    (c) stern   (d) wickedly cruel

67. **plaintive**
    (a) simple   (b) difficult
    (c) sad   (d) disrespectful

68. **platitude**
    (a) party   (b) overused expression
    (c) obedience   (d) underpaid worker

69. **precursor**
    (a) forerunner   (b) weapon
    (c) clown   (d) enemy

70. **prodigious**   (a) tiny   (b) favorable
                          (c) enormous   (d) sad

71. **purloin**   (a) vomit   (b) steal
                          (c) reject   (d) prove

72. **quixotic**   (a) practical   (b) modest
                          (c) fanciful   (d) spoiled

73. **refractory**   (a) absurd   (b) disobedient
                          (c) lazy   (d) vicious

74. **relentless**   (a) unyielding   (b) pitiful
                          (c) sleepy   (d) without money

75. **reminiscence**   (a) attack   (b) revolt
                          (c) memory   (d) circumstance

76. **reprove**   (a) escape   (b) remember
                          (c) capture   (d) rebuke

77. **repudiate**   (a) say again   (b) reject
                          (c) pretend   (d) cultivate

78. **revere**   (a) respect   (b) shut
                          (c) look back   (d) open

79. **rhetorical exaggeration** (a) understatement   (b) tumor
                          (c) overstatement   (d) giant

80. **sabotage**   (a) float   (b) secretly destroy
                          (c) cure   (d) balance

81. **sarcasm**   (a) mockery   (b) support
                          (c) poverty   (d) lack of effort

82. **satire**   (a) ridicule   (b) garment
                          (c) savagery   (d) promise

83. **sonorous**   (a) resounding .   (b) sorrow
                          (c) confused   (d) cheerful

84. **soporific**   (a) fat   (b) causing sleep
                      (c) muscular   (d) causing pain

85. **spoonerism**   (a) manners   (b) wisdom
                      (c) agony   (d) verbal blunder

86. **stagnate**   (a) be sure   (b) be idle
                      (c) be precise   (d) be cautious

87. **stolid**   (a) warm   (b) unemotional
                      (c) shivering   (d) explosive

88. **suave**   (a) bearded   (b) ridiculous
                      (c) unyielding   (d) sophisticated

89. **sybarite**   (a) philosopher (b) scientist
                      (c) tyrant   (d) pleasure seeker

90. **tabulate**   (a) strike   (b) prevent
                      (c) calculate   (d) despise

91. **tawdry**   (a) difficult   (b) showy and cheap
                      (c) informative (d) kind and helpful

92. **thwart**   (a) hinder   (b) suffocate
                      (c) speed up   (d) release

93. **tirade**   (a) storm   (b) verbal attack
                      (c) exhaustion   (d) cruel leader

94. **toady**   (a) circus   (b) cook
                      (c) flunky   (d) critic

95. **tribute**   (a) cruelty   (b) argument
                      (c) movement   (d) honor

96. **utilitarian**   (a) practical   (b) imaginary
                      (c) modest   (d) boastful

97. **vanguard**   (a) follower   (b) leadership
                      (c) protection   (d) pleasure

98. **vengeful**   (a) revengeful   (b) merciful
                          (c) complaining   (d) forgetful

99. **vulnerability**   (a) decision   (b) thought
                          (c) ridicule   (d) weakness

III. This exercise reviews those words which were derived from the word parts at the end of the individual chapters.

1. **abrogate**
   - (a) explain
   - (b) abolish
   - (c) calculate
   - (d) say again

2. **allude**
   - (a) perform
   - (b) kill
   - (c) stand up
   - (d) refer indirectly

3. **anarchy**
   - (a) peace
   - (b) disorder
   - (c) ruler
   - (d) religious leader

4. **arrogant**
   - (a) mild
   - (b) helpful
   - (c) energetic
   - (d) proud

5. **assent**
   - (a) agree
   - (b) disagree
   - (c) correct
   - (d) prove wrong

6. **avert**
   - (a) help
   - (b) prevent
   - (c) memorize
   - (d) repeat

7. **capitalize**
   - (a) lecture
   - (b) rule
   - (c) warn
   - (d) profit from

8. **capitulate**
   - (a) torture
   - (b) plunge
   - (c) fly
   - (d) surrender

9. **concede**
   - (a) improve
   - (b) deteriorate
   - (c) give up
   - (d) take back

10. **consensus**
    - (a) odor
    - (b) agreement
    - (c) prevention
    - (d) laughter

11. **decapitate**
    - (a) reveal
    - (b) hide
    - (c) behead
    - (d) discover

12. **delude**
    - (a) save
    - (b) give back
    - (c) mislead
    - (d) depend

13. **derogatory**
    - (a) negative
    - (b) positive
    - (c) exceptional
    - (d) possible

14. **diction**   (a) flight   (b) choice of words
    (c) muscle growth   (d) table manners

15. **dissension**   (a) harmony   (b) opinion
    (c) quarreling   (d) leadership

16. **dissent**   (a) agree   (b) disagree
    (c) correct   (d) prove wrong

17. **divert**   (a) turn aside   (b) fall down
    (c) raise up   (d) unify

18. **durable**   (a) pleasant   (b) exceptional
    (c) innocent   (d) lasting

19. **duration**   (a) hardship   (b) lack of support
    (c) promotion   (d) period of time

20. **duress**   (a) relaxation   (b) force
    (c) bride   (d) willingness

21. **edict**   (a) private sin   (b) public shame
    (c) public sin   (d) public command

22. **elude**   (a) build   (b) educate
    (c) escape   (d) pray

23. **endure**   (a) solve   (b) help, protect
    (c) promote   (d) exist, last

24. **hierarchy**   (a) peak   (b) ranked system
    (c) father   (d) criminal

25. **indict**   (a) accuse   (b) escape
    (c) show   (d) confuse

26. **insensible**   (a) unhealthy   (b) unnatural
    (c) unable to read   (d) unaware

27. **insensitivity**   (a) lack of reason   (b) lack of sensitivity
    (c) nonsense   (d) extreme sensitivity

28. **intercede**
(a) explain fully   (b) question
(c) prevent   (d) ask for another

29. **interlude**
(a) trap   (b) gap between events
(c) battle   (d) salvation

30. **interrogate**
(a) enter   (b) question
(c) explode   (d) cultivate

31. **jurisdiction**
(a) decision   (b) willingness
(c) presentation   (d) legal authority

32. **malediction**
(a) blessing   (b) ornament
(c) curse   (d) lost treasure

33. **matriarch**
(a) builder   (b) map
(c) stadium   (d) female ruler

34. **monarch**
(a) ruler   (b) nutrition
(c) friend   (d) opposition

35. **obdurate**
(a) stubborn   (b) sensitive
(c) lost   (d) skillful

36. **patriarch**
(a) storm   (b) male leader
(c) examination   (d) attraction

37. **per capita**
(a) per person   (b) for adults only
(c) uneven   (d) before sunrise

38. **precedent**
(a) prayer   (b) example
(c) monument   (d) female athlete

39. **prelude**
(a) introduction   (b) conclusion
(c) game   (d) servant

40. **prerogative**
(a) question   (b) statement
(c) privilege   (d) secret

41. **presentiment**
(a) expectation   (b) gift
(c) surprise   (d) wickedness

42. **recapitulate**
    (a) remove   (b) eat
    (c) summarize   (d) grow up

43. **recede**
    (a) move forward   (b) move backward
    (c) stay still   (d) move sideways

44. **revert**
    (a) return   (b) leave
    (c) invent   (d) communicate

45. **secede**
    (a) join   (b) withdraw
    (c) enlarge   (d) shrink

46. **sensual**
    (a) open   (b) profitable
    (c) bitter   (d) pleasure-loving

47. **sententious**
    (a) profitable   (b) full of proverbs
    (c) guilty   (d) nervous

48. **sentiment**
    (a) execution   (b) wealthy
    (c) poverty   (d) feeling

49. **subvert**
    (a) recognize   (b) overthrow
    (c) challenge   (d) reinforce

50. **vertigo**
    (a) health   (b) wealth
    (c) madness   (d) dizziness

BIBLIOGRAPHY

Most collegiate and unabridged dictionaries provide etymologies for words. Enclosed in brackets, these etymologies either precede or follow the definition. I particularly like the etymologies in *Webster's New World Dictionary* and the first edition of *The American Heritage Dictionary*. Space limitations, however, necessitate that dictionary etymologies be extremely compressed. There are also four standard modern etymological dictionaries: *The Barnhart Dictionary of Etymology, Klein's Comprehensive Etymological Dictionary of the English Language, Origins — A Short Etymological Dictionary of Modern English*, and *The Oxford Dictionary of English Etymology*. The etymologies in these dictionaries are also compressed rather than narrative, although *Barnhart* avoids bewildering abbreviations and is the most accessible to the non-specialist. The *Oxford English Dictionary* stands in a class by itself. It is a monumental work that contains a wealth of contextual illustrations to trace the evolution of words. Anyone interested in words should become acquainted with this work. What follows is a partial list of popular books that leisurely and entertainingly present fascinating etymologies for the general reader.

The American Heritage Dictionary Editors. *Word Mysteries & Histories*. Boston: Houghton Mifflin Company, 1986.

Asimov, Issac. *Words from History*. Boston: Houghton Mifflin Company, 1968.

Ciardi, John. *A Browser's Dictionary*. New York: Harper and Row, 1980.

_____. *Good Words to You*. New York: Harper and Row, 1987.

_____. *A Second Browser's Dictionary*. New York: Harper and Row, 1983.

Evans, Ivor H., ed. *Brewer's Dictionary of Phrases & Fables*. New York: Harper and Row, 1981.

Freeman, Morton S. *The Story Behind the Word*. Philadelphia: ISI Press, 1985.

Funk, Charles Earle. *Thereby Hangs a Tale*. New York: Harper & Row, 1950.

Funk, Wilfred. *Word Origins and Their Romantic Stories*. New York: Bell Publishing Company, 1950.

Garrison, Webb B. *Why You Say It*. New York: Abingdon Press, 1955.

Heller, Louis G., Alexander Humez, and Malcah Dror. *The Private Lives of English Words*. Detroit: Gale Research Company, 1984.

Hendrickson, Robert. *The Dictionary of Eponyms*. New York: Stein and Day, 1985.

_____. *The Facts on File Encyclopedia of Word and Phrase Origins*. New York: Facts on File Publications, 1987.

Limberg, Peter R. *Stories Behind Words*. New York: The H. W. Wilson Company, 1986.

McDonald, James. *Wordly Wise*. New York: Franklin Watts, 1985.

Morris, William and Mary Morris. *Morris Dictionary of Word and Phrase Origins*. New York: Harper and Row, 1977.

Shipley, Joseph T. *Dictionary of Word Origins*. Totowa, NJ: Littlefield, Adams, and Company, 1967.

Webster's Word Histories. Springfield: Merriam-Webster Inc., 1989.

Index

Words with exercises are in *italics*; the 100 core words are in **boldface**.